Editor
Mary S. Jones, M.A.

Cover Artist
Delia Rubio

Editor in Chief
Karen J. Goldfluss, M.S. Ed.

Illustrator
Bob Seal

Art Production Manager
Kevin Barnes

Imaging
Leonard P. Swierski

Publisher

Mary D. Smith, M.S. Ed.

WRITE from the START!

Grades 6-8

Writing Lessons

Writing Models & Activities

PRACTICE WRITING...
- Narratives
- Information Reports
- Poems
- Recounts
- Descriptions
- Speeches
- Explanations
- Procedures
- Research Projects

...and more!

Teacher Created Resources

Author

Kristine Brown

Teacher Created Resources, Inc.
6421 Industry Way
Westminster, CA 92683
www.teachercreated.com

ISBN: 978-1-4206-8074-4

© 2008 Teacher Created Resources, Inc.
Made in U.S.A.

Teacher Created Resources

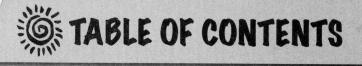

TABLE OF CONTENTS

Write from the Start! Writing Lessons helps students with the kind of writing they do every day. Each lesson looks at a different type of writing. Some are imaginative text types, such as narratives and poems. Others are factual text types, such as reports and explanations.

All lessons begin with a sample text, which serves as a lesson model or for students to use as a reference when applying a strategy to their own writing. It is important that the text and special features of the sample models are read and discussed with students. (Note: Many of the sample texts used throughout the book have been written by students, which will make them even more enjoyable for your students to read and analyze.)

After the sample model has been introduced, students can work through the activities that follow. These give them guidance and practice in writing a similar type of text. The first activities in each lesson ask students to focus on the context of the sample model and reflect on what they read and how it was written. Additional activities direct students to the grammar and punctuation used in the model and how these apply to the text. Lessons also include activities that help students with vocabulary meaning and spelling. Every lesson ends with a "Your Turn to Write" section, where students apply what they have learned. This can serve as a reflection or assessment tool for each lesson.

In addition to the space provided on the activity pages of this book, it is recommended that students have their own journals or writer's notebooks. These can be used for some of the writing activities at the end of most lessons, where students may wish to extend their writing. A journal or notebook is also a good place for students to add references (illustrations, advertisements, photographs, research information, etc.) that they collect for future writing.

If you plan to use all of the lessons in the book, it is best to work through the book from Lesson 1 to the end. This will allow students to build on skills from one lesson to the next. However, each lesson can be taught independently. You may even wish to focus on a group of lessons that meet specific needs or standards. In either case, the format of this book allows for flexibility.

☀ MEETING STANDARDS

The activities in this book meet the following writing standards, which are used with permission from McREL. Reading standards are also met by the "What Did You Read?" and "How Is It Written?" sections of each lesson; however, those standards are not listed below.

Copyright 2006 McREL. Mid-continent Research for Education and Learning.
Address: 2250 S. Parker Road, Suite 500, Aurora, CO 80014
Telephone: 303-377-0990 Website: *www.mcrel.org/standards-benchmarks*

Standard 1.   Uses the general skills and strategies of the writing process

1.   Prewriting: Uses a variety of prewriting strategies (Pages 19, 20, 27, 28, 34, 35, 42, 43, 49, 55, 56, 62, 63, 64, 70, 71, 77, 78, 79, 82, 83, 84, 85, 87)
2.   Drafting and Revising: Uses a variety of strategies to draft and revise written work (Pages 12,13,19, 20, 26, 27, 28, 33, 34, 35, 40, 42, 43, 49, 55, 56, 62, 63, 64, 70, 71, 77, 78, 79, 82, 83, 84, 85, 87)
3.   Editing and Publishing: Uses a variety of strategies to edit and publish written work (Pages 12, 13, 18, 19, 20, 27, 28, 34, 35, 42, 43, 45, 49, 55, 56, 58, 62, 63, 64, 70, 71, 77, 78, 79, 84, 85, 87)
4.   Evaluates own and others' writing (Pages 7, 15, 22, 30, 37, 45, 51, 58, 60, 61, 66, 73)
5.   Uses content, style, and structure appropriate for specific audiences and purposes (Pages 15, 18, 22, 37, 51)
6.   Writes expository compositions (Pages 6, 29, 36, 44, 57, 65, 70, 71, 72, 80, 81, 82, 83)
7.   Writes narrative accounts, such as short stories (Pages 14, 20, 50, 84, 85)
8.   Writes compositions about autobiographical incidents (Pages 19, 55, 56)
9.   Writes biographical sketches (Pages 12, 13)
10. Writes persuasive compositions (Pages 57, 63, 64, 77, 78)
11. Writes compositions that address problems/solutions (Pages 29, 72)
13. Writes business letters and letters of request and response (Pages 36, 42, 43)

Standard 2.   Uses the stylistic and rhetorical aspects of writing

1.   Uses descriptive language that clarifies and enhances ideas (Pages 21, 22, 24, 26)
2.   Uses paragraph form in writing (Pages 10, 30, 61)
3.   Uses a variety of sentence structures to expand and embed ideas (Pages 17, 24, 48)
4.   Uses explicit transitional devices (Pages 7, 60, 73

Standard 3.   Uses grammatical and mechanical conventions in written compositions

1.   Uses pronouns in written compositions (Pages 47, 48, 66)
2.   Uses nouns in written compositions (Pages 9, 47)
3.   Uses verbs in written compositions (Pages 22, 32, 47, 68)
4.   Uses adjectives in written compositions (Pages 34, 39)
5.   Uses adverbs in written compositions (Page 75)
6.   Uses prepositions and coordinating conjunctions in written compositions (Page 53)
8.   Uses conventions of spelling in written compositions (Pages 8, 16, 23, 31, 38, 46, 52, 54, 59, 67, 74)
9.   Uses conventions of capitalization in written compositions (Pages 69, 76)
10. Uses conventions of punctuation in written compositions (Pages 10, 18, 25, 33, 40, 48, 54, 69, 75, 76)
11. Uses appropriate format in written compositions (Page 69)

Standard 4.   Gathers and uses information for research purposes

2.   Uses library catalogs and periodical indexes to locate sources for research topics (Page 49)
3.   Uses a variety of resource materials to gather information for research topics (Pages 12, 13, 41, 49, 62, 70, 87)
4.   Determines the appropriateness of an information source for a research topic (Pages 49, 70)
5.   Organizes information and ideas from multiple sources in systematic ways (Pages 49, 71)
6.   Writes research papers (Pages 49, 70, 71)
7.   Uses appropriate methods to cite and document reference sources (Page 86)

YOUR TURN TO WRITE (cont.)

Goal or task (What were you trying to do? Who was involved? What was the overall plan or idea?)

_____

_____

_____

_____

Steps taken (What did you do? In what order? Remember to number the steps.)

_____

_____

_____

_____

_____

_____

_____

_____

_____

_____

_____

Evaluation (What did you learn? What did the procedure prove? Did you enjoy the experience?)

_____

_____

_____

_____

_____

_____

_____

② Think of something you have built or made—by yourself or with others. Here are some suggestions:
- furniture
- an insect trap
- a garden
- an ant farm
- a bridge
- a meal for your family
- a treehouse
- a kite
- a campfire

Using the same headings above, outline your procedural recount on your own paper. Remember: we want to know what you did and what worked and didn't work. Then rewrite it neatly after you have checked for grammar, punctuation, and spelling.

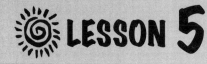

LESSON 5 — Writing a Letter of Opinion

In a **letter of opinion**, your aim is to convince the reader of your point of view using facts and logical arguments. A letter of opinion is a kind of editorial or persuasive writing.

STRUCTURE

LANGUAGE

Date and your address*

March 23, 2004

35 WXXXXXX Rd.
Balmain, FL 20357

Name, title, and address of person you are writing to

Ms. Sandra Nori
City Council Member
22 NXXXXXXX St.
Balmain, FL 20357

Polite, respectful language

Greeting

Dear Ms. Nori,

Personal language

Introduction to topic of letter, reason for writing, and point of view

My name is Joe Brown. I am 11 years old and I live in Balmain, Florida. I am writing to you because I love skateboarding, just like all my friends in the area you're in charge of. We need your help because a lot of adults in this area have tried to stop a skateboard park from being built downtown. They think young people will just gather there and make a mess. I think they're being mean and selfish.

Opinion adjectives

Logical arguments to support opinion

There are many good reasons for a skateboard park. First, skateboarding is a lot of fun for kids. Also, it will improve their skill and fitness and keep them out of trouble. Besides, a skateboard park would be a great place to make new friends. THIS WOULD BE GREAT FOR THE COMMUNITY!

Connectives to link ideas

Personal experiences to support opinion

I have skated at the Avalon Skateboard Park with some good friends. It's a great park designed by the local skateboarders, where big kids help little kids learn to skateboard, and where parents are happy to take their kids because it's a safe place.

Ending— repeating purpose of letter

If you can help put this skateboard park in, us kids will be very grateful.

Mostly formal language; but some informal language is also acceptable

Closing showing respect

With best wishes and lots of hope,

Joe Brown

Name and signature

Joe Brown

* We have blocked out and altered the actual addresses for privacy reasons.

🌀 WHAT DID YOU READ?

① What does Joe want Ms. Nori to do? _____

_____

② Circle the best answer. How does Ms. Nori have the power to help?
   a. She is an adult.
   b. She is a famous skateboarder.
   c. She is a city council member.

③ Circle the best answer. Who has stopped the skateboard park from being built, according to Joe?
   a. the people downtown
   b. adults who live in the area
   c. young people who make a mess

④ How many arguments does Joe put forward to support his opinion? _____

⑤ Which argument do you think is Joe's strongest, and why? _____

_____

⑥ Name one good point about the Avalon Skateboard Park. _____

_____

🌀 HOW WAS IT WRITTEN?

① Joe writes, "I love skateboarding, <u>just like all my friends</u>," "we need your help," and "<u>us kids</u> will be very grateful." Why do you think he does this? Circle the best answer.
   a. because his friends won't write letters
   b. because there are many children in the area
   c. because he wants to show he is not the only one who feels this way

② Joe lists many good reasons for building a skateboard park. Why do you think he put his last reason in capital letters? _____

_____

③ Personal experiences can be helpful in letters of opinion. Why do you think Joe thought it would help to mention his experience of the Avalon Skateboard Park? Circle the best answer.
   a. because it is his favorite place to skate and his parents like it, too
   b. because it is an example of a skateboard park that has been good for the community
   c. because it has been designed by local skateboarders

④ Circle the best answer. Why do you think it is a good idea to repeat the purpose of the letter at the end?
   a. to remind Ms. Nori in case she has forgotten
   b. to be polite
   c. to make his letter more persuasive

⑤ Do you think that Ms. Nori would be influenced by Joe's letter? Why or why not? _____

_____

SPELLING AND MEANING

Word Box	there	skateboard	friends	area	built
	their	reasons	improve	because	downtown
	they're	dangerous	community	designed	grateful

The word box contains three words that are often confused: **there**, **their**, **they're**.

- **There** means a place (e.g., over there). It is also for expressions like **there is**.

  Example: There are many good reasons for a skateboard park.
               You can USUALLY replace **there** with **here** and the sentence still makes sense.

- **Their** means "of them" (shows possession).

  Example: Also it will improve their skill and fitness (the skill and fitness of them).
               You can USUALLY replace **their** with people's names.

- **They're** means "they are."

  Example: They're being mean and selfish.
               You can ALWAYS replace **they're** with "they are."

① Choose **there**, **their**, or **they're** to use in these sentences.

   a. The girls would like _____ soccer team to win the competition.

   b. _____ playing at the local sports center.

   c. _____ are three good arguments for building an outdoor pool.

   d. I think _____ would be many people with the same opinion.

   e. _____ playing all _____ games over _____.

② **Antonyms** are words that have opposite meanings (e.g., **dangerous** and **safe**). Many antonyms are made by adding a prefix (e.g., **un**, **in**, **im**). Can you make the antonyms of these words by adding one of these prefixes?

   a. grateful _____   **b.** significant _____

   c. selfish _____   **d.** mobile _____

   e. perfect _____   **f.** personal _____

   g. polite _____   **h.** impressive _____

   i. active _____   **j.** adequate _____

   k. direct _____   **l.** effective _____

③ Many words are made by combining two words. The new word is a **compound word**. What compound words can you make by adding a word *before* or *after* the following words?

   a. board: _____

   b. snow: _____

   c. surf: _____

   d. wind: _____

GRAMMAR—OPINION ADJECTIVES

In letters of opinion, we often use adjectives that clearly show what that opinion is. For example, we might say that a local council decision is *great*, *terrific*, or *beneficial*. Of course, other people might call the same decision *ridiculous*, *useless*, or *harmful*.

These kinds of adjectives are called **opinion adjectives**. They are useful because they can influence the reader to agree with our point of view.

However, we need to use them with care—especially negative ones. They can give the impression that we are very emotional about the issue and so not thinking clearly. They can also be insulting—for example, if you say someone's idea is *stupid* or *idiotic*.

① Underline the adjective that tells the writer's opinion in each sentence below.

    a. The ramp would be a sensible way to use the money saved when the pool closed.

    b. The beautiful land behind my house is home to many kinds of wildlife.

    c. A new school library would be a brilliant way to get more kids to read.

    d. The parade is the most entertaining part of New Year's Day.

    e. Making the old tennis courts into a parking lot is a very boring idea.

② It is a good idea to vary the opinion adjectives that you use. Below are some words you could use instead of the opinion adjectives at the top of the column. Can you unscramble them? (The first letter is in **bold**.)

GOOD (e.g., plan, action, idea)	**BAD** (e.g., plan, action, idea)	**BEAUTIFUL** (e.g., building, landscape)	**UGLY** (e.g., building, landscape)
PSOTIEVI	**S**UESSEL	**L**ORGOUSI	**N**UATTRCATVIE
BRLLNTIAI	**U**NELPHFUL	**G**GROSEOU	**R**ETOLVGNI
SEULUF	**S**HKCONGI	**T**TAARCTEIV	**U**NEAPSLANT
XECLLENTE	**G**ENATVIE	**D**IDSLPEN	**E**TRRBLIE
LCVERE	**F**LUHARM	**G**AMNIFITENC	**S**IDGSTUING

PUNCTUATION—IT'S/ITS

It's and *its* are easy to confuse, but just remember these two things:

• *It's* ALWAYS ALWAYS ALWAYS means "it is" or "it has." ("It has" is less common.)

• *Its* is a word meaning "belonging to it" (just like **hers** means "belonging to her").

    Examples: It's a great park. (= It is a great park.)

                     It's been there for two years. (= It has been there for two years.)

                     I have an idea for its location. (= I have an idea for the location of it.)

So, use *it's* only if you can replace it with "it is" or "it has" and the sentence still makes sense.

①   Fill in the blanks below with *it's* or *its*.

    a. I believe _____ a really terrible plan.

    b. The group wants you to know _____ honest opinion.

    c. Most people who object to _____ construction don't know the facts.

    d. One thousand people say _____ an excellent place for a skatepark.

    e. _____ success will depend on _____ size, _____ design,

       and _____ location.

    f. _____ been talked about for long enough. _____ time for action.

CAN YOU HELP?

Joy wrote this letter to the editor of her local newspaper, but the order of her sentences has been mixed up. Can you put them back in the right order? Number them from 1 to 5.

    Dear Editor,

a. ____ In nearly every basketball game, someone slips and falls. There have been some serious injuries because so many people have slipped.

b. ____ Many people have complained about this before, and I think it's time someone did something about it.

c. ____ This should not keep happening. Someone should do something about it. They should rip up the old court and lay down new concrete.

d. ____ In fact, you could even ask one of my friends who tripped in a game and twisted her knee. She had to have an operation to put it back in place. She couldn't play for the rest of the season. It is very painful, and she has to use crutches.

e. ____ I am writing to complain that the Lapstone basketball courts are in a terrible condition. There is sand and dirt everywhere and small holes all over.

    Joy Tarasenko, Glenbrook

With permission, Joy Tarasenko and Blue Mountains Gazette

PUZZLE TIME

How much do you know about where sports are played? You'll find a few places in this crossword. You may need your dictionary or the Internet to help you.

Across:
3. Joe wants one of these built into the skateboard park.
6. You might have one of these in your backyard.
7. Lots of 6 Across together make an _____ center.
8. Might be made of grass or wood or a synthetic surface
9. You need two wheels for this speedy place beginning with V.
13. Another speedy place—but this time you will be on skates.
14. Ten pins are used in the sport played in this place.
16. A boat race or a series of boat races
17. This word is used in many sports. You might be familiar with one with obstacles.

Down:
1. Horses run around this, but humans do, too, in other sports.
2. A big place used for athletics and other major events
4. What the person on the mound in baseball does
5. If you want to snow ski, hit the _____.
6. Take a big jump into this and sand will fly.
10. Another word for a golf course
11. An egg-shaped place for sport or just running around
12. You will find parallel bars, rings, and trampolines here.
13. Bullets fly at the shooting _____.
15. Many indoor games are played on this.

☼ YOUR TURN TO WRITE

> **TIP FOR ELECTRICALLY EFFECTIVE LETTER WRITERS**
> When writing a letter to persuade someone to do something, remember to be polite as well as clear. You do not want the person to be insulted by the words you use. If the person is insulted, he or she is unlikely to agree with you or do what you want.

① Writing opinion letters is one way that ordinary people can influence what happens in their neighborhood, community, state, or country. Imagine that you wanted to write about the issues below. Who would you write to? Draw lines from the issue to the person or organization. (There may be more than one answer.)

a. A plan to close the local swimming pool   principal

b. People dumping trash into a local river   local newspaper

c. People throwing cigarette butts on the street   major newspaper

d. A plan to build an airport in your city   local council member or mayor

e. Extending summer vacation   school district superintendent

f. The need for new facilities (e.g., library, buildings, sports areas) at your school   government official

② Choose one of the above topics that interests you most to write a letter of opinion about. Use your own ideas and imagination to complete the letter outline below and on the next page. (Just make up a name for the person you are writing to if you do not know it.)

_____ (Today's date and your address)

_____

_____

_____ (Title/address of person you are writing to)

_____

_____

Dear _____,

I am writing about _____

_____

_____

_____

I think/I don't think _____

_____

_____

_____

_____

☀ YOUR TURN TO WRITE (cont.)

Here are _____ very good reasons. _____

_____

_____

_____

_____

_____

_____

_____

_____

_____

_____

This issue is really important to me and _____

so I hope _____

_____

_____

_____

_____

Thank you.

Yours sincerely,

_____

③ I am sure there is an issue in your local area that affects you (e.g., sports or other facilities for young people). Write a letter to the local newspaper or to your local council member giving your opinion. Use your own paper.

Remember:
- Write the date, your address, and the title and address of the person you are writing to.
- Say why you are writing.
- State your opinion clearly.
- Give some reasons to support your opinion.
- Add any personal experiences that support your opinion.
- Conclude by repeating why you are writing.
- Close with words that show your thanks and respect.

You will need to write your letter out again very neatly, and make sure the spelling, punctuation, and grammar are correct before you send it.

In an **information report**, your aim is to give your audience factual information on a topic. Many reports are about groups of things (e.g., stars), but some are about one particular thing (e.g., the moon).

STRUCTURE

LANGUAGE

Introduction to topic—often a definition or the way the topic is classified

Information organized by sub-topics, in paragraphs and under headings

Topic sentences to help us understand main ideas

Sometimes **explanations** of how or why things happen

Factual information, not your opinions or personal experiences

Conclusion (not always needed)

Special, "technical" words to talk about the topic

Often **passive forms of verb** to talk about processes

Definitions or explanations of terms readers might not understand

Usually **present tense of verbs** ("timeless present")

Mainly **factual adjectives**

Topic word (stars, a star) repeated to link ideas

STARS

What are Stars?

Stars are huge spheres of flaming gas. They are like huge nuclear furnaces. They throw out enormous quantities of light, heat, and other forms of energy. The heat is unimaginable to us—a core temperature of around 18 million degrees Fahrenheit. However, not all stars have the same amount of heat, and the difference can be seen by their color. The hottest stars shine blue and after that, in order of heat, they shine white, yellow, orange, and then red.

Our Sun

Our Sun is a star. It looks bigger to us than all the other stars in the sky, but this is only because it is the closest (about 93 million miles away) and the other stars are much farther away. The next nearest, Alpha Centauri, is 4.3 light years away. (One light year is the distance that light travels in one year.) That means it is more than 25 trillion miles away.

How Stars are Born

A star starts out as a cloud of hydrogen gas and dust. It begins to form when gravity makes it collapse, pulling the dust together. As it collapses, it begins to rotate and heat up. When the temperature gets high enough in the core (many millions of degrees) to set off nuclear reactions, it produces an enormous amount of energy, and the star begins to shine. These reactions are the same as in hydrogen bombs, only billions of times more powerful.

How Long Stars Live

Astronomers have observed many stars at different stages and pieced information together to get a typical star's lifespan. However, not all stars live for the same length of time. That depends on their size. The biggest stars have short, but spectacular lives. Middle-sized stars, like our own Sun, shine less brightly and die quietly, but they live longer—more than 5 billion years. The lightweight stars glow weakly, but may have a life measured in hundreds of billions of years.

How They Die

A star begins to die when it runs out of hydrogen (its fuel). The helium core shrinks while its outer layers expand. Dying stars can sometimes produce strange phenomena such as supernovae (the result of massive stars exploding violently and brilliantly in the sky) and black holes (the result of massive stars collapsing and creating an area from which no light can escape).

Astronomers are constantly learning more about stars thanks to powerful telescopes, such as the Hubble Space Telescope, and space satellites that are able to travel farther and farther into our vast universe.

✺ WHAT DID YOU READ?

① True or False?

    a. All stars give out the same amount of heat. _____

    b. The Sun is the biggest star in our galaxy. _____

    c. The main gas that fuels stars is hydrogen. _____

    d. Big stars live the longest. _____

    e. We are still learning more about stars. _____

② The nuclear reaction that produces stars is compared to _____.

③ What does the color of stars tell us? _____

④ What unit of measurement is used to talk about huge distances? _____

⑤ Circle the best answer. Stars are born . . .
    a. when they run out of hydrogen and collapse.
    b. when hydrogen and gas heat up and set off a nuclear reaction.
    c. when they get to a temperature of 15 million degrees.

✺ HOW WAS IT WRITTEN?

① Why do you think the writer defined "stars"?
    a. because the reader might not have seen any stars
    b. because stars are very important objects in our universe
    c. because the reader might not know exactly what stars are

② The writer repeats the word **star** or **stars** throughout the report in order to connect all the different facts. Underline each **star** or **stars** in the text and the headings. How many did you find altogether? _____

③ The information in "Stars" is clearly organized under headings. Under which headings would you add the three facts below?

    a. Letters are used to classify stars. W is for the hottest blue star class. _____

    b. Light takes eight minutes to reach us from the Sun. _____

    c. Some stars become what are known as "red giants" as they die. _____

④ The writer uses H _ _ _ _ _ _ S, P _ _ _ _ _ _ _ _ _ S, and

    T _ _ _ _ S _ _ _ _ _ _ _ _ _ to help us follow the main ideas.

⑤ These sentences were in the first report draft. Why do you think the writer took them out?
    I love to look up at the stars at night.
    Stars are more interesting than planets, in my opinion.

_____

⑥ These special scientific words are in the report. Check those that are defined. Circle those that you would have liked definitions for.

nuclear _____   Fahrenheit _____   black holes _____

light years _____   supernovae _____   gravity _____

☼ SPELLING AND MEANING

Word Box	sphere	enormous	unimaginable	million	difference
	collapse	gravity	rotate	temperature	enough
	powerful	spectacular	measured	phenomena	massive

① When we add endings to words (**suffixes**), we don't hear the suffix vowel sound very clearly and this can make them difficult to spell. Write the words from the word box that work with the suffixes below, and then learn them using the **look–say–cover–write–check** method (see page 8).

    a. –ous _____   **b.** –ful _____

    c. –ar _____   **d.** –ive _____

    e. –able _____   **f.** –ure _____

② Choose a word from the word box to complete each sentence.

    a. If Earth did not _____ on its axis, we would not have night and day.

    b. Earth is about 93 _____ miles from the Sun.

    c. A high-jumper on the moon could jump over a house because of the weak _____.

    d. There is a big _____ between the night sky of the Northern Hemisphere and that of the Southern Hemisphere.

    e. A star the size of our Sun requires 50 million years to grow, from the beginning of the _____ to maturity.

③ **Sphere** and **phenomena** have a **ph** spelling for the "f" sound. (**Phenomena** is the plural of **phenomenon**.) Can you match these **ph** words to their meanings? Use a dictionary if needed.

    a. phenomenon   round, three-dimensional object or shape

    b. phantom   a person who seeks wisdom or enlightenment

    c. phase   imaginary bird in ancient stories

    d. philosopher   ghostly apparition

    e. phoenix   an observable fact or event

    f. phony   short group of words

    g. prophet   stage in a process

    h. phrase   prize or award

    i. sphere   someone who predicts the future

    j. trophy   fake, unreal

④ An astronomer is a scientist who studies the universe and space. Can you fill in the missing letters to make other kinds of scientists?

    a. B __ __ __ __ IST: a scientist who studies plants

    b. B __ __ __ O __ IST: a scientist who studies living things

    c. __ E __ L __ __ IST: a scientist who studies rocks and Earth's structure

    d. __ __ Y __ ICIST: a scientist who studies natural laws of physical matter and energy

    e. C __ __ __ IST: a scientist who studies chemical reactions

GRAMMAR—SINGULAR AND PLURAL AGREEMENT

Read the following sentences aloud:

A star <u>starts</u> out as a cloud of hydrogen gas and dust. ✓
A star <u>start</u> out as a cloud of hydrogen gas and dust. ✗

Stars <u>are</u> huge balls of flaming gas. ✓
Stars <u>is</u> huge balls of flaming gas. ✗

If the subject is **singular**, you need a **singular verb**. If the subject is **plural**, you need a **plural verb**. **The subject and verb must agree.**

Now look at how these sentences continue, using pronouns instead of the noun subjects.
The pronouns are shown in *italics*.

A star <u>starts</u> out as a cloud of hydrogen gas and dust. *It* <u>begins</u> to form. As *it* <u>collapses</u>, *it* <u>begins</u> to rotate and heat up. ✓

Stars <u>are</u> huge balls of flaming gas. *They* <u>are</u> like huge nuclear furnaces. *They* <u>throw</u> out enormous quantities of light, heat, and other forms of energy. ✓

Always check that your subjects and verbs **agree in singular or plural**. Also check that the **pronouns** used to refer back to the subjects **agree**.

Correct the singular/plural agreement where needed in these sentences. The first one has been done for you.

                                               They   come

a. Comets are frozen, lifeless bodies. ~~It~~ only ~~comes~~ to life when near the Sun's heat.

b. Meteors are sometimes called "shooting stars," but it is not really a star.

c. Some meteors are colored—mostly blue and white, though it might sometimes be red or green.

d. A communication satellite bounce signals from one point on Earth to another point.

e. Galaxies are vast clusters of thousands of millions of stars. It is classified according to its shape.

f. Telescopes magnify distant objects in the night sky. It uses lenses and mirrors to make things appear closer and larger.

> ### DID YOU KNOW?
> There is a word to describe the figure 1 followed by 100 zeros! It is "googol."

PUNCTUATION—PARENTHESES

We use **parentheses to include extra bits of information**, especially definitions and measurements. Look at these examples from "Stars":

. . . but this is only because it is the closest (about 25 trillion miles away) . . .

. . . is 4.3 light years away. (One light year is the distance that light travels in one year.)

Can you add the extra bits of information from the box to the sentences below, enclosing them in parentheses?

which is 93 million miles away   opposite to Earth   around 870 degrees Fahrenheit named after the Roman goddess of love   only 405 miles less in diameter

a. Earth is the third planet from the Sun _____.

b. Venus _____ is Earth's closest neighbor.

c. Venus is also the closest in size to Earth _____.

d. Venus spins from west to east _____.

e. Venus is the hottest planet in the solar system _____.

CAN YOU HELP?

Can you correct these mistakes with singular and plural agreement? The wiggly lines will help you.

People used to think comets were fireballs, but that is not correct. It is actually a frozen, lifeless body most of the time. They have solid centers of dirty ice surrounded by gas. It only comes to life when it comes near the Sun, because the Sun heats them up and releases gases trapped inside. These gases form the tails of comets. The tails of comets can be millions of kilometers long—it is really only because of its tail that we see comets at all. Comets orbit the Sun just like planets, but its orbit are far greater and so it lasts much longer. Some take thousands of years to complete their orbit. The most famous comet is Halley's Comet, which comes around about every 76 years. The last time was in 1986, and it is expected to return in 2061.

PUZZLE TIME

① Can you unscramble these SPACE words?

a. SARM __ __ __ __

b. CTMEO __ __ __ __ __

c. STAROTAUN __ [ ] __ __ __ __ __ __

d. REJPUIT __ __ __ [ ] __ __ __

e. MTEEOTIRE __ [ ] __ __ __ __ __

f. NEVSU [ ] __ __ __ __

g. TASRUN __ __ __ __ __ __

h. USURAN [ ] __ __ __ __ __

i. TUNEPEN [ ] __ __ __ __ __ __

j. CERMRYU __ __ [ ] __ __ __ __

k. RATHE [ ] __ __ __ __

l. XAGLYA __ __ __ __ __ __

② Now write the letters from the boxes in activity 1 and unscramble them to get a word that covers them all! __ __ __ __ __ __ __ __ __ → _____

☼ YOUR TURN TO WRITE

TIPS FOR MARVELOUSLY METEORIC WRITERS

You usually write reports after reading or watching something, so you'll often have more information than you need. Don't try to include everything—just select the most important and interesting facts. Also, don't just copy an information text—use your own words. Then make a plan. Organize your facts under headings before you start your draft.

---

① Here are some facts about galaxies. Use the information below and your own research to draft a report about galaxies on your own paper. Use headings such as "What are galaxies?" "How were they formed?" "What do they look like?" and "Our own galaxy: the Milky Way" to help you organize your information.

- Change the order of the information around if you think you need to.
- Use your own words where possible.
- Leave out any information you do not understand.
- Explain anything the reader might not understand.

Galaxies

- vast clusters of thousands of millions of stars, planets, gases, and dust
- like islands in an ocean of space
- held together by gravity
- hundreds of millions of galaxies
- every galaxy a very long way from all the others
- formed during the Big Bang about 15,000 million years ago
- formed from lumps of matter that resulted from the Big Bang
- classified according to shapes
- most common type is spiral—like a pinwheel—but some are oval, some are irregular
- our galaxy—the Milky Way—spiral-shaped
- our solar system is near the edge of our galaxy
- contains about 100 billion stars—still producing new ones
- about 100,000 light years across
- astronomers think an enormous black hole is at the center of our galaxy
- although Milky Way is huge, is only a small part of the Universe—one of millions of similar galaxies

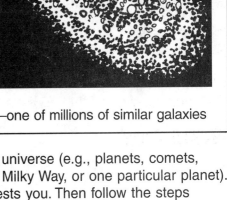

---

② Now write a report on another topic related to space and the universe (e.g., planets, comets, meteorites, the moon, the Sun, space travel, black holes, the Milky Way, or one particular planet). Look through some books first to find a topic that really interests you. Then follow the steps below to write an information report on your topic. Draft your report on your own paper.

- Do some research to find out some facts about your topic.
- Decide what you want to include in your report (you can't include everything).
- Organize your facts into three or four sub-topics.
- Begin your draft report with a definition of your topic.
- Draft your sub-topic paragraphs.
- Revise your draft and check your spelling, punctuation, and grammar. Look out especially for singular/plural agreement. Be sure that you have kept your report factual and have not included your own opinions.
- Rewrite your report neatly.

LESSON 7 — Writing a Description

The aim of a **description** is to give your reader a clear and vivid picture of a person, thing, place, or scene. It is often part of a longer text, such as a narrative. This text is a description of a scene.

STRUCTURE

LANGUAGE

This description is from a novel written as the diary of a young English boy named David Bellamy. It is 1807, and David has been sent to live in Sydney Town with his uncle and aunt after his parents have died. He has traveled as a passenger on a convict ship. The excerpt describes the scene at the docks a day after his ship has landed. The convicts are starting to come off the ship, and David is waiting outside a building where he is to meet his uncle.

Introduction to topic: who, what, when, where

Description of the scene: physical things (objects, buildings, landscape); actions and behaviors; sounds; atmosphere

Paragraphs to separate different parts of the scene or different time periods

Concluding comment (not always necessary)

Common nouns to name people or things

Phrases and clauses to add detail

Interesting, expressive verbs

Language that creates clear pictures of people and things

Usually **present-tense verbs**

Descriptive adjectives

Thursday, December 17th

I am writing this while I sit in front of the building, and already I am receiving strange glances. A soldier sitting on a pile of ropes studied me as I sat down and undid the lid of my ink. He seemed satisfied and promptly took a swig from his bottle, closed his eyes, and is now sleeping. Each person who wanders past me stares. There is a woman just now, with a baby wrapped in a shawl, and she calls to another to come and see what I am doing. I ignore them. A boy about my age is fishing at the edge. He has just caught a large silver fish, and he flicked it up high in the air. It landed beside him and flopped about as he tried to take the hook from its mouth. Blood splashed on his hands. Even now, in the bag behind him, I see squirming and imagine that fish gasping for its last breath of air.

The convicts are coming off. They are strangely quiet now, staring at the wide expanse of sky, not seen by them since we crossed the Line some months back. Perhaps, like me, they cannot believe how blue this sky can be and how harsh is the Southern sun. But I have grown used to it these past days. I know a splash of water on my skin or clothes will dry in moments. They are pitiful in their rags. They stagger forth, and many stumble and fall, clutching at their fellows when they reach solid land. It is as if the Earth still moves under foot, so accustomed are we to the movements of the ocean waves. Soldiers are everywhere, easy to see in their bright red jackets, although some are torn and, in places, more brown than red. They stamp up and down the length of the area, shouting at the convicts and pushing those who move too slowly or who step away from the line. I cannot hear clearly the words the soldiers say, but their tone is rough and angry. A convict boy, no bigger than myself, catches my eye and says something, which I also cannot hear. He thrusts his arm forward in a wild gesture and twists his face, so I know his words are unkind. What can he have done to be sent to this place? The wretches are marched off, away from where I sit. I am hungry. I wish my Uncle would come.

From *My Story: The Rum Rebellion: The Diary of David Bellamy*, by Libby Gleeson, 2001. Text copyright © Libby Gleeson. First published by Scholastic Press, a division of Scholastic Australia Pty Ltd, 2001. Reproduced by permission of Scholastic Australia Pty Ltd

☼ WHAT DID YOU READ?

① In paragraph 1, what is the soldier doing? _____

What is the boy doing? _____

② In paragraph 2, which two groups of people are described? _____

What are they doing? _____

_____

③ Sometimes a writer does not give you all the information. You have to figure it out yourself. Answer these questions based on the information in the text.

a. Why do people stare at David and give him strange glances (what is he doing that might be unusual)? _____

b. Why is David more used to the sky and sun than the convicts are? _____

_____

c. What do you think "the Line" is? _____

d. Why do the convicts find it difficult to walk? _____

_____

e. Why is the young convict boy angry with David? _____

_____

④ The atmosphere is different in the two paragraphs.
a. Which paragraph suggests a dark, rather gloomy atmosphere? _____
b. Which paragraph suggests a bright, calm atmosphere? _____

☼ HOW WAS IT WRITTEN?

① David does not describe every single thing or person he sees. Instead he describes the most
I __ __ __ __ __ __ __ __ __ __ things and people. In paragraph 1, for example, he only

describes __ __ __ __ __ people.

② David gives a sense of the sounds, as well as the sights, of the scene.

a. What words tell us about the sound of the convicts? _____

b. What words tell us about the sound of the soldiers? _____

③ David chooses good verbs to show the action. Write two verbs used to describe . . .

a. what the fish does. _____

b. the way the convicts move. _____

c. the way the soldiers behave. _____

d. the gestures of the young convict boy. _____

④ **a.** Do you have a clear image of the scene after reading the description? (yes/no) _____

b. On your own paper, draw a picture of the scene.

SPELLING AND MEANING

Word Box	glances	soldier	promptly	swig	wanders
	wrapped	pitiful	stagger	stumble	clutching
	although	rough	thrusts	gesture	wretches

① Choose a word from the word box to complete each sentence. Then learn how to spell them using the **look–say–cover–write–check** method (see page 8).

a. The poor _____ had spent six whole months aboard the ship.

b. The woman stares at me and then _____ a book roughly into my face.

c. The man got his meaning across using only facial expressions and a hand _____.

d. It was _____ to see how thin and pale the convicts were.

e. The old man _____ aimlessly around the street, _____ a tiny leather bag to his chest.

f. The sick and injured _____ and _____ as they are pushed along.

g. The _____ was very _____ with the convicts.

h. _____ she was _____ in a shawl, she was shivering with the cold.

i. He had a _____ of rum and then _____ fell down at my feet.

② There are many vivid verbs in the English language to describe the way people walk or move. Here are some from the text:

stagger	stumble	stamp	march	squirm	flop	twist

Here are a few more:

dash	shuffle	stomp	glide	prowl	pace	slip	totter	lumber	hobble	scurry	slither

Can you match any of the verbs above to the person or animal below? Use your dictionary to help you. (You might find more than one verb for each.)

a. a very, very old person: _____

b. a dancer on stage: _____

c. a person waiting to hear important news: _____

d. a person in a hurry: _____

e. a huge ogre or monster: _____

f. a skater or acrobat: _____

g. an animal waiting to catch prey: _____

h. a person with an injury: _____

i. a person on stilts or high heels: _____

j. a mouse: _____

k. a snake or lizard: _____

GRAMMAR—ADJECTIVAL AND ADVERBIAL PHRASES

We sometimes want to give our readers a clearer picture about the people and things (the nouns) we write about—**whose, with what, where, what like, about what, what kind, why.**

Examples: A boy <u>about my age</u> is fishing . . .

They are pitiful <u>in their rags</u>.

There is a woman just now, <u>with a baby wrapped in a shawl</u>, . . .

Phrases that add information to nouns are called **adjectival phrases**.

At other times we want to give our readers a clearer picture about what the people and things are doing (the **verbs**)—**when, where, how, why.**

Examples: A soldier sitting <u>on a pile of ropes</u> studied me.

He thrusts his arm forward <u>in a wild gesture</u> . . .

Phrases that add information to verbs are called **adverbial phrases**.

All the phrases above begin with **prepositions**—such as ***on***, ***in***, ***with***, ***without***, ***about***, ***up***, ***at***, ***across***, ***from***, ***to***, ***beside***, ***next to***, ***like***, ***for***—but not all phrases do.

① Underline the adjectival or adverbial phrases in these sentences and draw a box around the prepositions. Some may have more than one set.

   a. Their hair is knotted with dirt and straw.

   b. The trip across the oceans was harsh and long.

   c. Many of the women by the docks were carrying small children. (two phrases)

   d. Children played quite happily on the pebbly shore.

   e. I felt sick with grief and loneliness.

   f. Travelers led their weary horses to the water troughs outside the public house. (two phrases)

② Add phrases to these sentences to give more information about the underlined nouns or verbs. Use the prepositions in parentheses.

   a. The old man wore a <u>coat</u> (with) _____

   b. I could see a long <u>line of children</u> (outside) _____

   c. The animals <u>were</u> hungry and thirsty (after) _____

   d. The trees provided no real <u>protection</u> (from) _____

   e. The sky <u>was</u> heavy (with) _____

   f. The prisoners <u>looked</u> longingly (at) _____

PUNCTUATION—COMMAS TO ADD DESCRIPTIVE DETAIL

We often need a **comma before and after a descriptive detail** to make our meaning clear, especially when the detail comes in the middle of a sentence.

Examples: There is a woman just now, with a baby wrapped in a shawl, and she calls . . .

A convict boy, no bigger than myself, catches my eye . . .

However, we don't always need a comma. For example, we don't need one when the detail identifies the person or thing.

Example: A soldier sitting on a pile of ropes studied me as I sat down.

In this sentence, we are identifying which soldier we are talking about—that is, the one sitting on the pile of ropes.

A good way to help you know if a comma is needed is to read the sentence out loud with commas and without commas and see which way sounds better.

Insert commas where needed in these sentences. Remember to first read them out loud.

a.   The boys hoping to reach the top by sundown pushed on in the fading light.

b.   A small girl hat tucked under her arm smiled shyly at us.

c.   There are ten men in the room all sitting around a small table and they look up as we enter.

d.   My uncle usually a rough-spoken man gently asked the boy his name.

e.   The swimmers exhausted by their adventure flung themselves onto the riverbank.

f.   The students playing near the basketball courts are in trouble.

g.   The small children kept awake by the noise huddled together under the blankets.

h.   The old man his eyes flashing angrily refused to move.

i.   The boy looking this way is the thief.

CAN YOU HELP?

This student wrote a description of a parade in a letter to her friend while on vacation. However, she forgot to use any punctuation and she spelled several words incorrectly. Can you correct her writing? Rewrite the paragraph correctly on your own paper. Underline the words that you corrected.

I am siting here in a café in the town square wating for a parade to begin althogh the day is extremly cold the crowd is huge everone is very exited and very noisy as they wait for the parade to start I can here trumpets and drums the parade has begun leading the parade are peple on stilts waring bright-colored hats and floing capes one stumbels for a second before steadying up and continuing on the croud cheers the stilt-walkers are folowed by some very small childern their faces are painted with animel masks and they are cluching balloons in their hands now I can see young grils in bodysuits doing cartweels and tumbles the sene changes every minute each time a new group appears the crowd shouts out and cheers wildly the biggest cheer is given to the town band at the end of the parade and to a little boy playing a very big drum

PUZZLE TIME

Can you unscramble the words below? You'll find each one in the picture.

a. GGGBEAA _____   b. TYTJE _____

c. DCKE _____   d. PSSGAENRE _____

e. CHRONA _____   f. SMAT _____

g. RTHLOEOP _____   h. CTPAIAN _____

YOUR TURN TO WRITE

> **TIP FOR DYNAMICALLY DESCRIPTIVE WRITERS**
> When you describe a scene, don't include every single thing you can see. Describe only the things that are interesting or that you can describe in an interesting way. Give detail about these things to make the scene come alive.

① Let's try writing a short description of a familiar scene that involves a few people. If you are at home, go and find a place where you can sit comfortably and observe people (members of your family, neighbors, passers-by) going about their everyday activities. You might go to the kitchen, the family room, the balcony, the backyard, or the front porch, for example. If you are at school, stay in the classroom or go somewhere on the playground.

   a. Now imagine you are describing the scene for someone who has never seen it and knows nothing about it—perhaps as part of a diary entry or a letter. Take a few minutes to look around you. Think about these points, and then jot down your ideas around the questions below.

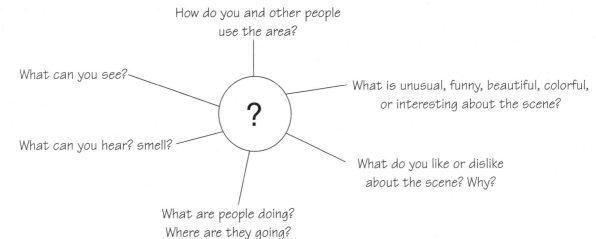

   b. Now you should be ready to write a draft of your description. Think about the questions you just answered above and write your description on your own paper. You could begin as David Bellamy did: "I am writing this while I sit . . ." Then rewrite your description neatly after you have proofread it.

⚙ YOUR TURN TO WRITE (cont.)

② Now write a description of any scene you like that has special importance for you. If you are not near the scene at the moment, you will have to depend on your imagination and your memories. Here are some suggestions:

- a place where you like to shop (e.g., the mall, street fair)

- a place where you like to read (e.g., the library, a bookstore)

- a noisy place (e.g., a busy restaurant, a concert)

- a place where you go for vacation (e.g., an amusement park, the beach, the mountains, a camping site)

- a new place you have moved to (e.g., a house, a street, a town, a country)

- the home of a friend or family member (e.g., your cousins' house, your grandparents' house)

- a port where boats of some kind come in (e.g., fishing boats, ocean liners)

Again, imagine you are writing your description as part of a diary entry or letter to be read by someone far away who knows nothing about the scene you are describing. Think about what they would find interesting.

Brainstorm ideas as you did in the previous activity before you start writing. Remember that you don't have to describe everything—just the most interesting things about the scene. Write your description on your own paper.

DID YOU KNOW?

Children as young as eight or nine years of age were sometimes transported to Australia in the late 1700s and early 1800s for small crimes. Most were orphans who had had to make their own way in the world from a very early age. *Oliver Twist* by Charles Dickens tells of young people in this situation.

When you give an **opinion speech**, your aim is to persuade your audience that your opinion is right and sensible. Because you want your audience to listen closely to what you are saying, you should also try to make it interesting and entertaining.

STRUCTURE

Greeting to audience

Introduction to topic and your point of view

Something to ***capture the audience's interest***

Series of arguments, given one at a time

Arguments developed with one or two examples or details

Conclusion repeats point of view and rounds off the talk

Thanks to audience for listening

ZOOS ARE NOT CRUEL PLACES. DO YOU AGREE?

Good morning, class. Last August, I visited the Melbourne Zoo in Australia while on vacation with my family. I saw a baby Sumatran orangutan. His birth was part of an international program to help the Sumatran orangutan survive as a species. At the moment these beautiful creatures are in danger of disappearing in the next 10 to 20 years.

Melbourne Zoo is a modern zoo. Like most modern zoos, it cares very much about animals. It is NOT a cruel place. You could certainly argue that zoos WERE cruel places in the past, but I don't believe you can argue that they ARE cruel places today.

In the past, zoos were exhibition parks. Their only purpose was to give humans pleasure by showing them wonderful, exotic creatures that they would otherwise never see. Because animals were only there for the benefit of humans like you and me, no one took much care of them. They were transported thousands of miles around the world, then locked up in small, bare, lonely cages. In those days, zoos were cruel.

These days, things are very different. The whole purpose of zoos has changed. Now zoos have three major purposes: education, conservation, and research. They aim to make animals better off everywhere. Because of this, the way animals are cared for is also different.

Firstly, education. Education is a big part of the activities at zoos. At Sydney's Taronga Park Zoo, for example, 130,000 school children attend special programs every year to learn about how animals behave and what they need to live. The aim is to make children more aware of animals now so that they will care about them when they are adults. It is the same in most zoos all around the world.

Secondly, conservation. Zoos play a major role in the protection and conservation of endangered species. The Sumatran orangutan is just one example of the many animals that are better off because of special breeding programs. I also heard about the Western Plains Zoo in Dubbo and learned about the black rhinoceros breeding program. Have you ever seen new baby animals being born like I did?

Lastly, research. Zoos are involved in many important research programs that help animals in captivity and in the wild. Recent research, for example, has shown that many intelligent animals benefit from being given puzzles to solve while in captivity, so now many zoos are providing mental challenges in their monkey enclosures.

Modern zoos care about animals first and people second. The people who work in them care about the animals' comfort, their freedom, and their survival as species. Zoos ARE NOT cruel places. I can't wait to go visit the ones here in our area! Thank you for listening.

Maria Masri

LANGUAGE

Talking about your ***own experience***

Capitals or highlighting to remind speaker to emphasize words

Talking directly to audience to make it more personal

Opinion adjectives

Interesting detail

Connectives to show that you are moving to a new point

Question to involve the audience

Sentences not too long and complicated

WHAT DID YOU READ?

① Does Maria agree or disagree with the statement that "zoos are cruel"? _____

② Complete the sentences. According to Maria . . .

    a. zoos of the past put _____ first, but modern zoos put _____ first.

    b. The purpose of zoos of the past was _____

    _____

    c. The three main purposes of modern zoos are _____

    _____

③ Circle the best answer. Zoos put on programs for children to . . .
    a. show them animals that adults don't usually see.
    b. make them care about animals now and when they are adults.
    c. teach them how animals behave.

④ Name one animal species mentioned that has been helped by special breeding programs.

_____

HOW WAS IT WRITTEN?

① In the first draft of her speech, Maria wrote the paragraph below as her first paragraph. Why do you think she changed it? _____

_____

> This morning I will talk about the difference between the past and the present. I will talk about the purpose of zoos today—education, conservation, and research—and how this has made them places where animals are very well treated.

② Circle the best answer. The main argument that ties all the smaller arguments together is:
    a. Zoos of the past were cruel, but zoos today are not.
    b. Zoos aim to educate people about animals.
    c. The main purposes of zoos are research, education, and conservation.

③ Maria organized her arguments and spoke about them one at a time. Can you put the arguments she covered in the order that she mentions them? (Write 1, 2, 3, 4, or 5.)

    zoos and research   _____   purpose of zoos today   _____

    zoos and education   _____   purpose of zoos in the past _____

    zoos and conservation   _____

④ Using **you**, **I**, and **we** and asking your audience questions are two ways to make your speech more personal and get your audience to listen. Look back at the speech and underline all the times Maria uses the word **you**. How many did you find? _____

⑤ How convincing do you find the arguments in the speech? (Check one)

    Very convincing   _____   Quite convincing   _____

    Not very convincing _____   Not at all convincing _____

    Give your reasons. _____

_____

SPELLING AND MEANING

Word Box	international	survives	species	disappearing	modern
	cruel	certainly	believe	purpose	pleasure
	protection	conservation	research	endangered	captivity

TIP FOR SPECTACULAR SPELLERS
Long words look hard but are often easier to spell than short ones because they are spelled the way they sound. Breaking words up into syllables helps to avoid leaving out letters (e.g., **con-ser-va-tion**).

① Slowly say the words in the word box aloud, breaking them into syllables. Write the words that have:
   a. one syllable _____
   b. two syllables _____
   _____
   c. three syllables _____
   d. four syllables _____
   e. the most syllables _____ How many syllables does this word have? ___

② In the words **certainly** and **species** the letter **c** is used for the **s** sound. This is called a "soft **c**." Choose the "soft c" words from the box below to complete each sentence.

science	recently	century	center	exceptions	excellent	celebrated

   a. In the 19th _____, animals in zoos were poorly treated.
   b. Research is very important in _____.
   c. Most modern zoos provide _____ care for the animals, but there are _____.
   d. _____, a local zoo _____ the birth of a baby zebra.

③ Can you draw lines between the matching synonyms below?

pleasure   vanish   disappear   aim   benefit   display   endangered

recent

merciless   advantage   cruel   research   exhibition   certainly

satisfaction   purpose   study   modern   definitely   threatened

④ Choose a word from the word box to complete each sentence.
   a. An _____ species is one that is in danger of becoming extinct in the next ten to twenty years.
   b. You have to _____ the topic to prepare a good speech.
   c. Breeding in _____ can help a species to survive.
   d. Poachers who kill for profit are one of the main dangers for many _____.
   e. Do you _____ that zoos care mostly about the animals?
   f. The program was _____, with many countries around the world participating.

✺ GRAMMAR—CONNECTIVES

Connectives are words that **show how your ideas are connected** from one sentence or paragraph to another. They are very important when you give an opinion in a speech or in writing.

In the speech about zoos, for example, the connectives *firstly*, *secondly*, and *lastly* showed that the speaker was listing a series of points—moving from one point to another. The connectives *in the past* and *these days* showed that she was contrasting two different time periods.

Look at these different kinds of connectives.

Listing a series of points	Adding new or extra information	Giving examples	Talking about different time periods	Contrasting ideas	Showing causes and results

first of all
to start with
next
firstly
secondly
finally
	also
	furthermore
	besides
	as well
	in addition
		for example
		for instance
			then
			now
			in the past
			these days
			at the moment
				however
				on the other
				  hand
				in contrast
				nevertheless
					so
					as a result
					therefore
					because of
					  this

Write the connectives below in the right spaces to show the connection between ideas in these sentences.

> as a result   firstly   for example   however   nevertheless   secondly

a. Most zoos these days take very good care of the animals. _____, it was not always this way.

b. Many breeding programs have been a great success. The white rhino, _____, was nearly extinct in the 1960s but is now back at safe levels.

c. A breeding program for the bald eagle has been in place for the last few decades.

_____, the bald eagle has recovered to numbers of 50 years ago.

d. Since 1984, rangers in Zimbabwe have worked hard to stop poachers from killing black rhinos.

_____, in that time, more than 1,170 rhinos have been killed.

e. I believe that zoos are cruel places. _____, animals must put up with human

beings all day. _____, there is absolutely no need for animals to be there.

✺ PUNCTUATION—HIGHLIGHTING

When you write out your speech, it is a good idea to **highlight** some words (with a highlighter, by underlining, or by writing in capital letters). This will remind you which words to **emphasize or say with special expression**. The best way to find out which words to highlight is to read your speech out loud beforehand.

Periods, commas, exclamation marks, and question marks also help you deliver a speech well. For example, they tell you when to pause, when to look up at your audience, and when to change your voice in some way.

✺ PUNCTUATION—HIGHLIGHTING (cont.)

① Read the paragraph from the zoo speech below out loud, emphasizing the words in capitals.

Melbourne Zoo is a modern zoo. Like most modern zoos, it cares very much about animals. It is NOT a cruel place. You could certainly argue that zoos WERE cruel places in the past, but I don't believe you can argue that they ARE cruel places today.

Did you notice how emphasizing these words helps to make the contrast between the past and the present clear?

② Now read these paragraphs from the zoo speech out loud and underline the words you would emphasize to get the main points across (only three or four in each paragraph).

In the past, zoos were exhibition parks. Their only purpose was to give humans pleasure, by showing them wonderful, exotic creatures that they would otherwise never see. Because animals were only there for the benefit of humans like you and me, no one took much care of them. They were transported thousands of miles around the world, then locked up in small, bare, lonely cages. In those days, zoos were cruel.

These days, things are very different. The whole purpose of zoos has changed. Now zoos have three major purposes: education, conservation, and research. They aim to make animals better off everywhere. Because of this, the way animals are cared for is also different.

✺ CAN YOU HELP?

This student wrote this paragraph for a speech arguing against killing animals for fur. Can you put the sentences into the order that makes the argument make sense? Use the connectives and other words in *italics* to help you.

a. _____ *They* buy them to look beautiful.

b. _____ Of course, *the people* who buy animal furs and skins *nowadays* don't buy them to keep warm and dry.

c. _____ Killing animals to make clothing is completely unnecessary *in this day and age*.

d. _____ *They* did not have the technology we have *these days* to keep ourselves warm and dry using other materials like cotton and synthetics.

e. _____ I wonder if *they* think about the poor animals killed in the process.

f. _____ *In the Stone Age*, humans had to kill animals for their fur and skin, because that was the only way they could survive.

DID YOU KNOW?
There are about 1,000 endangered species in the world today.

✺ PUZZLE TIME

How many of these zoo words can you find in the wordsearch?

zoo	protected	habitat	poaching	nature	control
conservation	endangered	vulnerable	threat	extinct	population
parks	species	wildlife	breeding	hunting	research

```
R B P E Q B W R E T R J I K H C Z I O P L F S
F W U R H A B I T A T T V H G F E Q E A I B M
U R E I N M L D L R E W N U O T Y B V E H Y U
E N D A N G E R E D X S D F L A I T B N Y I L
I L B P S R P O P U L A T I O N R T Y B V E W
P U Y G S Z X I O L F I T Y U R E S E A R C H
P R C M O A L B C E W R F F A S L R B F E O U
A O X N G R P R O T E C T E D U T R A T H W R
R Q A E L O Q E N T Y O D S A G B K G B T M O
K W R C T K I E T R T N T Y N I A Q M N L D B
S Y T R H L Y D R T Y S P E C I E S T R S E T
Q U U T R I Z I O R E E T Y F F X S D X K L I
L P I O E Y N N L R F R D G H J T L J H A P K
O K P G A Q A G R T A V A T S G I T Y U B V F
R S O F T W F M E G P A R F H U N T I N G K J
T A A S U D D G W Z G T H K G O C Q W E T H F
B E C D Y G H F Q F O I T J F I T A L H P R O
V F O Y Q M T S P S G O E Q A E M L T G I R E
W G L F P B L A M K D N A T U R E P E Q T U A
```

✺ YOUR TURN TO WRITE

TIPS FOR SERIOUSLY SOPHISTICATED SPEAKERS

It is not just how you write your speech that is important, it is how you deliver it to your audience. Here are some tips to help you:
- Write your speech on small cards.
- Look up from your cards as much as you can.
- Make eye contact with different people in the audience.
- Pause often to give your audience time to catch up. It is a good idea to write "STOP!" in big letters on your cards after every few lines.
- Speak loudly and clearly. Imagine that you are speaking to the person at the back of the room.
- Try not to be nervous. Smile at your audience. They will usually smile back and you will immediately feel better.

① Here are three points you could make in a speech to show that zoos are not cruel. Develop the points by giving an example (perhaps from your own experience of visiting zoos).

a. Zoos these days do everything possible to make animals feel at home.

_____

_____

_____

b. Zoos these days do everything possible to keep animals in good health.

_____

_____

_____

⊚ YOUR TURN TO WRITE (cont.)

c. More and more zoos are allowing the animals to roam free and enclosing the human visitors instead.

_____

_____

_____

② There is always more than one way to look at a topic, and it is a good idea to think of both sides when preparing a speech. In a debate, you are told which side of an argument you have to take, and it might not be the side you really agree with!

Imagine you were told to argue that zoos ARE cruel places. Read the arguments below and choose **only three** to use in a speech. Draft your speech in the space below and on the next page, and then rewrite it neatly using your own paper.

- Zoos take animals out of the natural web of life.
- Exposing animals to humans all the time has negative effects.
- The trapping of animals sometimes hurts or even kills animals.
- Animals in zoos are there for the entertainment of humans.
- Keeping animals in zoos is unnatural.
- There are still many zoos around the world that keep animals enclosed in small spaces.
- We don't need zoos to educate us. We can read about animals and watch wildlife programs.
- We have no way of knowing what animals feel.
- Most animal species in zoos are not endangered.
- Research can be done in the wild.

Introduction (Try to catch the audience's interest immediately. State the topic and your point of view.)

_____

_____

_____

_____

_____

_____

First argument (Show the audience you are moving to your first argument, state your argument, and develop it with an example.)

_____

_____

_____

_____

_____

_____

_____

_____

YOUR TURN TO WRITE (cont.)

Second argument (Show them you are moving on to your second point, state your argument, and develop it with an example.)

_____

_____

_____

_____

_____

_____

_____

_____

Third argument (Show them you are moving on to your third point, state your argument, and develop it with an example.)

_____

_____

_____

_____

_____

_____

_____

_____

Conclusion (Repeat your view and end your talk.)

_____

_____

_____

_____

_____

_____

_____

③ Following the same format from the previous activity, choose one of the topics below and write a 2-minute speech giving your opinion for or against. (Use your own paper.)
- Should people continue to be allowed to hunt certain animals for pleasure?
- Is it always worth saving animals from extinction?
- Should dog owners be legally obligated to walk their dogs?
- Should people who do not have outdoor yards be allowed to have dogs?

The aim of an **explanation** is to tell how or why something happens. Explanations are often about natural or scientific phenomena, processes, or events.

STRUCTURE

LANGUAGE

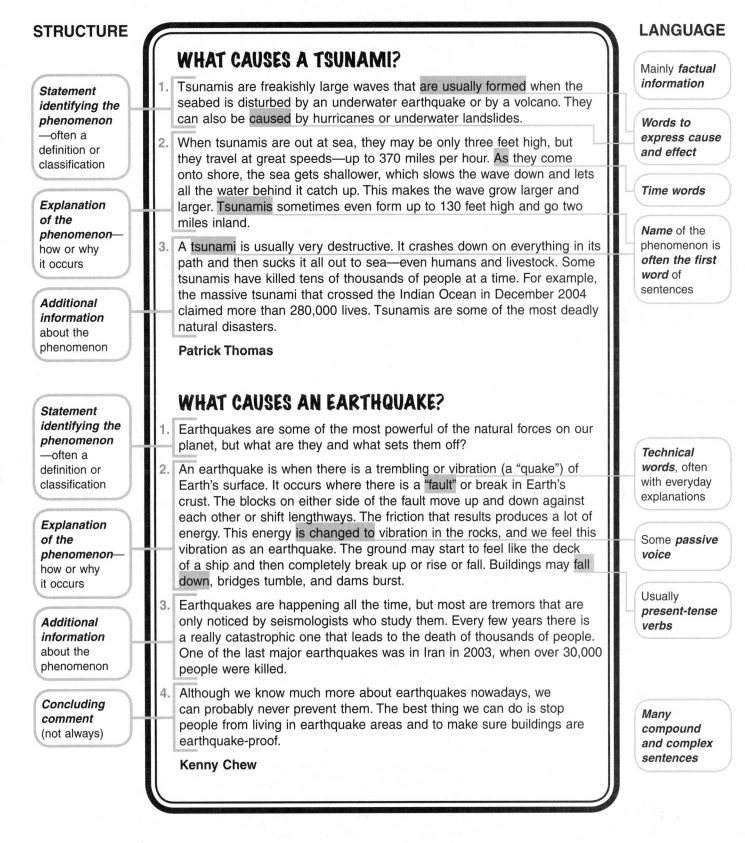

- Statement identifying the phenomenon—often a definition or classification

- Explanation of the phenomenon—how or why it occurs

- Additional information about the phenomenon

WHAT CAUSES A TSUNAMI?

1. Tsunamis are freakishly large waves that are usually formed when the seabed is disturbed by an underwater earthquake or by a volcano. They can also be caused by hurricanes or underwater landslides.

2. When tsunamis are out at sea, they may be only three feet high, but they travel at great speeds—up to 370 miles per hour. As they come onto shore, the sea gets shallower, which slows the wave down and lets all the water behind it catch up. This makes the wave grow larger and larger. Tsunamis sometimes even form up to 130 feet high and go two miles inland.

3. A tsunami is usually very destructive. It crashes down on everything in its path and then sucks it all out to sea—even humans and livestock. Some tsunamis have killed tens of thousands of people at a time. For example, the massive tsunami that crossed the Indian Ocean in December 2004 claimed more than 280,000 lives. Tsunamis are some of the most deadly natural disasters.

Patrick Thomas

- Mainly *factual information*
- *Words to express cause and effect*
- *Time words*
- *Name* of the phenomenon is *often the first word* of sentences

WHAT CAUSES AN EARTHQUAKE?

- Statement identifying the phenomenon—often a definition or classification

- Explanation of the phenomenon—how or why it occurs

- Additional information about the phenomenon

- Concluding comment (not always)

1. Earthquakes are some of the most powerful of the natural forces on our planet, but what are they and what sets them off?

2. An earthquake is when there is a trembling or vibration (a "quake") of Earth's surface. It occurs where there is a "fault" or break in Earth's crust. The blocks on either side of the fault move up and down against each other or shift lengthways. The friction that results produces a lot of energy. This energy is changed to vibration in the rocks, and we feel this vibration as an earthquake. The ground may start to feel like the deck of a ship and then completely break up or rise or fall. Buildings may fall down, bridges tumble, and dams burst.

3. Earthquakes are happening all the time, but most are tremors that are only noticed by seismologists who study them. Every few years there is a really catastrophic one that leads to the death of thousands of people. One of the last major earthquakes was in Iran in 2003, when over 30,000 people were killed.

4. Although we know much more about earthquakes nowadays, we can probably never prevent them. The best thing we can do is stop people from living in earthquake areas and to make sure buildings are earthquake-proof.

Kenny Chew

- *Technical words*, often with everyday explanations
- Some *passive voice*
- Usually *present-tense verbs*
- *Many compound and complex sentences*

WHAT DID YOU READ?

① What four natural events can cause tsunamis? _____

_____

② True or False?

   a. Tsunamis travel faster near the land. _____

   b. Tsunamis are bigger near the land. _____

   c. As the wave slows down, it gets bigger. _____

③ What is a "fault"? _____

④ Do you think tremors are small or large earthquakes? _____

⑤ Circle the best answer. Which of these word sequences shows how earthquakes happen?

   a. movement → friction → energy → vibration

   b. friction → movement → vibration → energy

   c. movement → energy → friction → vibration

HOW WAS IT WRITTEN?

① Explanations often include a definition of the phenomenon being explained. Underline the definition of *tsunami* in text 1 and *earthquake* in text 2.

② When writing explanations, you need to think about the best place to include your information.
   a. Where would you add this sentence to the first text? (Put an X in the text.)
      Tsunamis have nothing at all to do with tides.
   b. Where would you add these sentences to the second text? (Put an X in the text.)
      i. Electricity lines are cut, gas and water mains are ruptured, and fires break out, adding to the destruction.
      ii. The world's deadliest recorded earthquake occured in 1556 in central China, killing an estimated 830,000 people.

③ In explanations, we often begin sentences with the name of the phenomenon (e.g., *Tsunamis*, A *tsunami*, *Some tsunamis*) or with pronouns to replace these words (e.g., *They*, *It*). This helps our readers keep track of our ideas.
   a. Circle every time Patrick or Kenny use *tsunami* or *earthquake* at the beginning of their sentences.
   b. Underline every time they use the pronouns *it* or *they* at the start of sentences.

④ Did you find these students' explanations easy to understand? (yes/no) _____

   Would it have helped to have a diagram of what happens? (yes/no) _____

⑤ Draw a simple diagram (on your own paper) of one phenomenon to show what happens—a tsunami building up as it gets closer to shore or an earthquake beginning beneath Earth's surface.

DID YOU KNOW?
It is estimated that there are 500,000 detectable earthquakes in the world each year! 100,000 of those can be felt, and 100 of them cause damage.

✹ SPELLING AND MEANING

Word Box	disturbed	earthquake	volcano	caused	hurricanes
	landslides	shallower	destructive	livestock	eruption
	vibration	occurs	friction	tremors	catastrophic

① Put the words from the word box into alphabetical order. Remember: look at the second, third and fourth letters (and so on) if the first letters are the same. (Learn those you are not sure of using the **look–say–cover–write–check** method from page 8.)

_____   _____

_____   _____

_____   _____

_____   _____

_____   _____

_____   _____

_____   _____

② Fill in the blanks with words from the word box.

a. _____ are the same as avalanches.

b. The floods _____ terrible damage to the coastal towns.

c. The wild winds _____ the animals.

d. The _____ of the volcano was totally unexpected.

e. Some areas have not had earthquakes, but they have had many earth _____.

f. The _____ between the two rocks creates energy.

③ Many adjectives that describe disasters are made from (or *derived* from) nouns (e.g., **catastrophic** is derived from **catastrophe**). Fill in the blanks to make the adjectives below. Write the nouns they are derived from next to them.

a. DIS __ __ TR __ __ S   _____

b. TR __ GI __   _____

c. DE __ T __ UC __ IVE   _____

d. TE __ __ IB __ __   _____

e. HO __ __ IF __ C   _____

f. SH __ __ __ ING   _____

g. D __ V __ ST __ TING   _____

h. C __ L __ MITOUS   _____

⊚ SPELLING AND MEANING (cont.)

④ The word *tsunami* comes from the Japanese language, *tsu* meaning "harbor" and *nami* meaning "wave." Do you know these other words of Japanese origin?

a. Paper folding: O __ __ __ __ __ I

b. A wide-sleeved gown: K __ __ __ __ O

c. A method of self-defense: K __ __ __ __ E

d. Singing along to music with words on a screen: K __ __ __ __ __ E

⊚ GRAMMAR—ACTIVE AND PASSIVE VOICE

When writing, we can choose either the **active voice** or **passive voice** of verbs. Look at these sentences:

An underwater earthquake <u>disturbs</u> the seabed. (active voice)
The seabed <u>is disturbed by</u> an underwater earthquake. (passive voice)

The information in both sentences is the same, but the **emphasis** or **focus** is different. In the first sentence, the emphasis is on the *underwater earthquake* and what it does (it disturbs something). In the second, the emphasis is on the *seabed* and what happens to it (it is disturbed by something).

We usually put the words we want our readers to focus on at the beginning of the sentence. We use the **active voice** when we want the focus on **who or what is doing something** and what it does (e.g., <u>An underwater earthquake disturbs</u> the seabed).

We use the **passive voice** when we want the focus on the **thing that something is done to** and/ or what is done to it (e.g., The <u>seabed is disturbed by</u> an underwater earthquake). We also use the passive voice when it is not important to say who or what is doing something.

Example: Sometimes survivors <u>are found</u> days after the earthquake occurs. (We're interested in the *survivors*, not who found them.)

All the sentences below are in the active voice. Can you change them so that they are in the passive voice? Begin with the underlined words. The first one has been done for you.

a. Earthquakes usually disrupt <u>road and rail transportation</u>.

<u>　Road and rail transportation are usually disrupted by earthquakes.　</u>

b. People living in tall buildings felt <u>the tremors</u>.

_____

c. Scientists use <u>seismographs</u> to measure vibrations.

_____

d. Smaller aftershocks sometimes follow <u>the main quake</u>.

_____

e. Two earthquakes on the seabed triggered <u>waves up to 33-feet high</u>.

_____

f. Seismologists use <u>the Richter Scale</u> to measure earthquakes.

_____

g. Scientists have identified <u>earthquake "hot spots."</u>

_____

PUNCTUATION—QUOTATION MARKS FOR TECHNICAL WORDS

We often use **quotation marks** when we use a **technical word**, but only the first time we use it.

Example: It occurs where there is a "fault" or break in Earth's crust. The blocks on either side of the fault move up and down against each other or shift lengthways.

This tells our reader that the word has a special, technical meaning in this context.

We don't usually use quotation marks for the name of the phenomenon we are explaining (e.g., tsunami). It is usually clear that this is a technical term by its use in the title of the text.

Extra! Do you know why Kenny used quotation marks for "quake"? He wanted to show that the "quake" part of "earthquake" means vibration. He used the quotation marks to show that he was taking this part of the word out of the full word, for this special reason.

Put the technical words in quotation marks where needed in this paragraph from a text explaining glaciers. Remember to use them the first time (only) you come across the technical word.

At the back end of a glacier, high up in the mountains, is a large basin called the neve. The neve is where the snow builds up and gets packed in ice. The long, middle part of the glacier is called the trunk. The ice from the neve slowly flows downhill and adds to the trunk of the glacier. Eventually, ice from the trunk arrives at the front end of the glacier—the terminal. This is where the glacier melts and comes out as a stream or river. As the glacier moves downhill it moves over humps and around bends in the valley. This causes the glacier ice to crack and buckle. The cracks formed are called crevasses. When the glacier flows down a steep drop, an icefall is formed. An icefall is like a waterfall but is made of glacier ice.

> ## COMMAS
> It can be difficult to know when to use commas in the kind of long sentences you often need when explaining things. Sometimes a comma will seem necessary, but at other times it will interrupt the flow of ideas. Sometimes it will not matter if you use a comma or not. A good way to tell if you need a comma or not is to read your writing out loud and with expression. You will often hear whether you need a comma to make your ideas clear when you pause during the reading.

CAN YOU HELP?

Can you help put in commas, periods, and capitals where you think they are needed in this second paragraph about glaciers? Remember, reading it out loud will help you.

Glaciers are like huge rivers of ice that come sliding down from the mountains high up in the alps layers and layers of snow build up and get pressed together into ice as the ice gets heavier and heavier it starts to slide downhill this moving ice is called a "glacier" sometimes glaciers gradually expand and move forwards down the valleys into the sea but at other times they gradually shrink and move backwards up into the mountains when the front end of a glacier moves forwards we say it is "advancing" and when it moves backwards we say it is "retreating"

PUZZLE TIME

Can you write these disaster words into the no-clue-crossword spaces so that they all fit?

| TORNADO | TYPHOON | CYCLONE | AVALANCHE | FLOOD |
| HURRICANE | VOLCANO | BLIZZARD | EARTHQUAKE | DROUGHT |

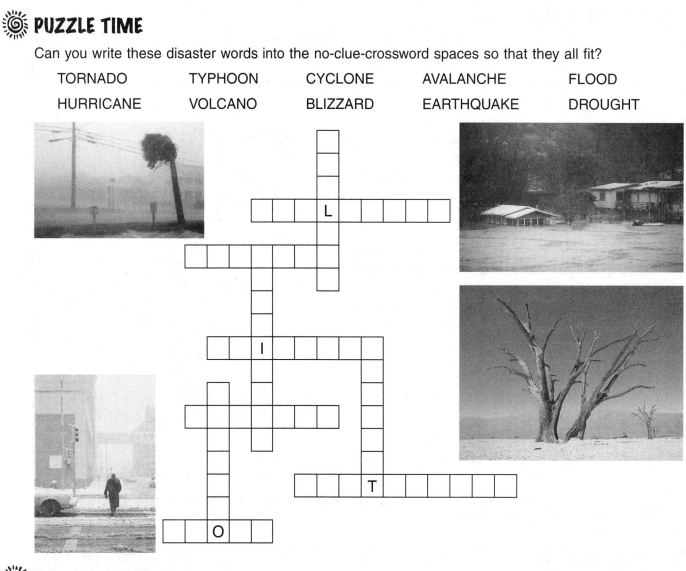

YOUR TURN TO WRITE

> **TIPS FOR PHENOMENAL WRITERS**
> When writing an explanation, be sure you understand what you are trying to explain. Ask people questions (your teacher, your parents, for example) and research your topic thoroughly to be sure what happens when, why, and how. Then try to explain the process verbally to someone else to check if your explanation is clear BEFORE you put it in writing.

① In the box on the next page is some information in note form about tornadoes and a simple diagram. Read through the notes and look at the diagram. Then do additional research about tornadoes using books, encyclopedias, or the Internet, if possible. After you get a good understanding about tornadoes, write an explanation on your own paper following this order:
- statement of phenomenon
- explanation of how or why
- extra information
- concluding comment (optional)

Note: You don't have to include all the facts and information that you learn. Include only the most important and interesting points.

✹ YOUR TURN TO WRITE (cont.)

- Tornadoes—also known as "twisters"
- Funnel-shaped tubes of rapidly spinning air—like huge swirling ropes of air
- Few hundred meters across
- May strike quickly, with little or no warning
- Average forward speed is 30 MPH, but may vary from stationary to 70 MPH
- Usually happen when thunderstorms around—energy in huge thunderclouds spirals downwards—just like what happens as water spirals down the drain in the bath
- Under right conditions—warm, humid air starts to rise upwards—at same time, very strong winds blow in opposite directions around rising air
- Whirling effect starts—whirling pushes air from center (like clothes being spun in a washer)
- Leaves a core of low pressure in center—low pressure like a powerful vacuum—sucks up everything in path
- Very destructive—can suck the walls of a house outwards so it collapses
- 500 to 600 tornadoes each year in US
- *Twister*—popular film

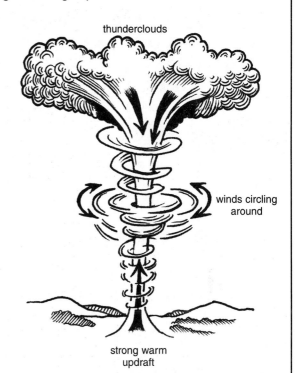

thunderclouds

winds circling around

strong warm updraft

② For extra practice, choose one of the natural phenomena from the box below and write a short explanation using your own paper.

- Do some research to find out about the phenomenon. Talk to someone if you need help to understand.
- Write a plan that includes the important things you need to mention.
- Draft your explanation following the same stages in the previous activity. Keep it simple—don't include every single detail.
- Read through your explanation as you go to make sure it is clear and makes sense.
- Give it to someone else to read when you finish your draft. Make changes if they did not understand something or if you left out important information.
- Proofread for spelling, punctuation, and grammar.
- Write your explanation out properly and draw a picture to go with it.

What causes hail?
How does snow form?
What causes brushfires?
What causes rainbows?
Why do avalanches happen?
What causes the greenhouse effect?

In a **discussion**, your aim is to present both sides of an issue (question) in a balanced way and then come to a conclusion.

STRUCTURE

LANGUAGE

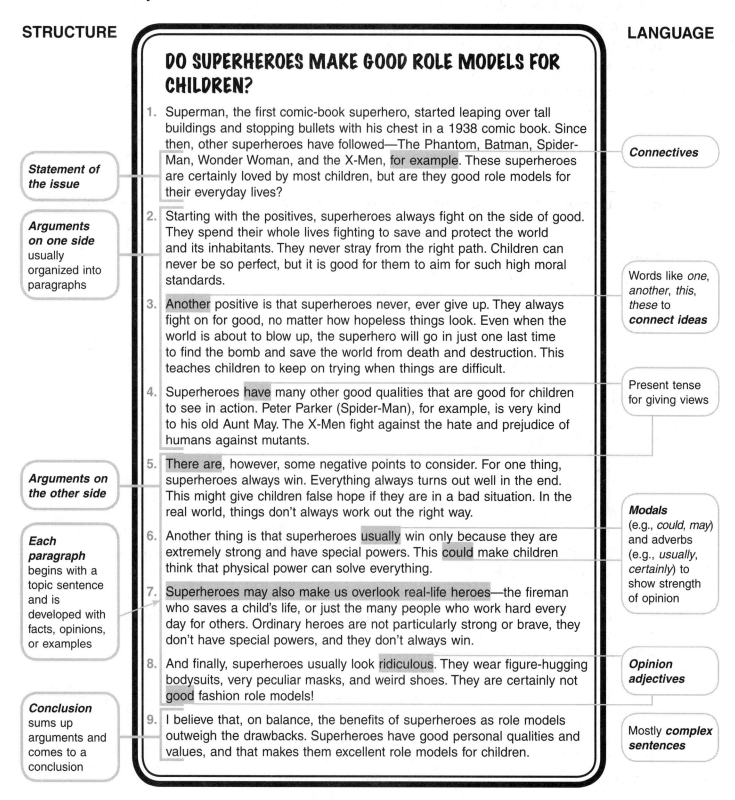

DO SUPERHEROES MAKE GOOD ROLE MODELS FOR CHILDREN?

1. Superman, the first comic-book superhero, started leaping over tall buildings and stopping bullets with his chest in a 1938 comic book. Since then, other superheroes have followed—The Phantom, Batman, Spider-Man, Wonder Woman, and the X-Men, for example. These superheroes are certainly loved by most children, but are they good role models for their everyday lives?

2. Starting with the positives, superheroes always fight on the side of good. They spend their whole lives fighting to save and protect the world and its inhabitants. They never stray from the right path. Children can never be so perfect, but it is good for them to aim for such high moral standards.

3. Another positive is that superheroes never, ever give up. They always fight on for good, no matter how hopeless things look. Even when the world is about to blow up, the superhero will go in just one last time to find the bomb and save the world from death and destruction. This teaches children to keep on trying when things are difficult.

4. Superheroes have many other good qualities that are good for children to see in action. Peter Parker (Spider-Man), for example, is very kind to his old Aunt May. The X-Men fight against the hate and prejudice of humans against mutants.

5. There are, however, some negative points to consider. For one thing, superheroes always win. Everything always turns out well in the end. This might give children false hope if they are in a bad situation. In the real world, things don't always work out the right way.

6. Another thing is that superheroes usually win only because they are extremely strong and have special powers. This could make children think that physical power can solve everything.

7. Superheroes may also make us overlook real-life heroes—the fireman who saves a child's life, or just the many people who work hard every day for others. Ordinary heroes are not particularly strong or brave, they don't have special powers, and they don't always win.

8. And finally, superheroes usually look ridiculous. They wear figure-hugging bodysuits, very peculiar masks, and weird shoes. They are certainly not good fashion role models!

9. I believe that, on balance, the benefits of superheroes as role models outweigh the drawbacks. Superheroes have good personal qualities and values, and that makes them excellent role models for children.

Structure labels (left):

Statement of the issue

Arguments on one side usually organized into paragraphs

Arguments on the other side

Each paragraph begins with a topic sentence and is developed with facts, opinions, or examples

Conclusion sums up arguments and comes to a conclusion

Language labels (right):

Connectives

Words like *one*, *another*, *this*, *these* to **connect ideas**

Present tense for giving views

Modals (e.g., *could*, *may*) and adverbs (e.g., *usually*, *certainly*) to show strength of opinion

Opinion adjectives

Mostly **complex sentences**

WHAT DID YOU READ?

① Circle the best answer. What are *all* the positive arguments about?
   a. the qualities of superheroes
   b. the qualities of the stories they appear in
   c. how superheroes fight to save the world

② According to the writer . . .
   a. Why is it good for children to see superheroes always keeping to the right path?

   _____

   b. How might superheroes help children to keep on trying when they face difficulties?

   _____

   c. What is one difference about the way things happen in the world of superheroes and the real

   world? _____

③ Circle the best answer. Which argument for the negative is not serious?
   a. first   **b.** second   **c.** third   **d.** fourth

④ Does the writer conclude for or against the question? _____

   Do you agree or disagree? Give at least one reason. _____

   _____

HOW WAS IT WRITTEN?

① You must state the issue at the start of the discussion, but it is good to give some background to the issue first. This writer tells us H __ __   L __ __ __ comic-book superheroes have been around and the N __ __ __ __ of some well-known ones.

② The writer gives about the same number of arguments for and arguments against. Why do you think this is a good idea? _____

③ Circle the best answer. There are a few ways to sum up arguments in the conclusion. This writer . . .
   a. summarizes the arguments on the side she agrees with.
   b. mentions the main argument for and the main argument against.
   c. summarizes all the arguments on both sides.

④ Words like **one**, ***another***, ***other***, ***one other***, ***one more***, ***also***, and ***too*** help to link the arguments across the discussion. (They are a bit like the threads that sew up different pieces of material.) Underline these "thread" words at the start of paragraphs 3, 4, 6, and 7.

⑤ Check ✓ the things that helped you follow the whole discussion.

   Arguments for separate from arguments against _____

   Separate paragraphs for each argument _____

   Topic sentences _____

   "Thread" words _____

   Conclusion _____

SPELLING AND MEANING

Word Box	superheroes	whole	perfect	moral	standards
	positive	qualities	negative	prejudice	mutants
	particularly	ridiculous	benefits	drawbacks	balance

TIP FOR SIMPLY SUPERHEROIC SPELLERS
Don't rely ONLY on a computer spell-check to get the spelling right when you type. If you type the sentence "They spend their hole lives saving the world," the spell-check will not pick up that you incorrectly used **hole** (meaning "space") instead of **whole** (meaning "complete"). The spell-check only looks at the word, not the meaning of the word in the sentence. Be sure to use the grammar-check feature, as well, along with proofreading your writing carefully.

① Choose words from the word box to match the clues.
   a. opposite of *part* _____
   b. synonym for *advantages* _____
   c. synonym for *silly* _____
   d. synonym for *disadvantages* _____
   e. adjective describing something with no faults _____
   f. positive features or characteristics _____
   g. to do with good and bad behavior _____
   h. creatures produced by a genetic change _____
   i. an adverb meaning the same as *especially* _____
   j. rules of behavior _____
   k. an unfair opinion formed without thought or knowledge _____
   l. something used to weigh things _____

② For most words ending in a consonant **+ o**, add **es** to form the plural (e.g., **superhero →
   superheroes**). Some exceptions are **pianos**, **photos**, **solos**. Can you unscramble these
   −oes words?
   a. MOTTAOES _____   **b.** TOPTAOES _____
   c. CANLOVOES _____   **d.** CEHOES _____
   e. OSQMUITOES _____   **f.** ROTPEDOES _____
   g. GMANOES _____   **h.** REHOES _____

③ There are many words to talk about the arguments **for** and the arguments **against** in a
   discussion. Can you add the missing words to this table?

FOR	AGAINST
Advantages	
Pluses	
	Negatives
Benefits	D
Affirmative case (used in debating)	N case

GRAMMAR—MODALS AND ADVERBS

When we write discussions or editorials, we often need to show how strongly we believe something or how sure we are about what we say.

One way we do this is by using **modals** such as *can*, *might*, *may*, *could*, *will*, *should*, and *must* in the verb group.

> *Examples:* This <u>might</u> give children false hope if they are in a bad situation.
> Superheroes <u>may</u> also make us overlook real-life heroes.

Another way is by using **adverbs** such as *definitely*, *really*, *perhaps*, *maybe*, *surely*, *certainly*, *possibly*, *probably*, *likely*, *always*, *never*, *usually*, *often*, and *sometimes*.

> *Examples:* These superheroes are <u>certainly</u> loved by most children . . .
> . . . superheroes <u>usually</u> look ridiculous.

Often we use **modals and adverbs together** to show what we think.

> *Example:* Children can never be so perfect . . .

We can also show how strongly we feel by NOT using a modal.

> *Example:* <u>This teaches children to keep on trying.</u> (is stronger and more definite than)
> <u>This may teach children to keep on trying.</u>

Look at the sentences below. For each group, write:
- 1 for the strongest, most-certain opinion
- 3 for the weakest, least-certain opinion
- 2 for the opinion in between

a. The Phantom is definitely the best superhero ever. _____

The Phantom is probably the best superhero ever. _____

The Phantom may be the best superhero ever. _____

b. We should encourage children to watch films like *Spider-Man*. _____

We must encourage children to watch films like *Spider-Man*. _____

We could encourage children to watch films like *Spider-Man*. _____

c. Children could copy the behavior of superheroes. _____

Children are sure to copy the behavior of superheroes. _____

Children might possibly copy the behavior of superheroes. _____

d. Parents should always stop children from watching these shows. _____

Perhaps parents should stop children from watching these shows. _____

Parents should probably stop children from watching these shows. _____

PUNCTUATION—APOSTROPHE OF POSSESSION

We use an **apostrophe** to show that a person or thing **owns or possesses** another.

> *Example:* a <u>child's</u> life = the life <u>of a child</u>

People often get confused about when and where to use the apostrophe of possession, but it is really very simple.

When to use it
You MUST use the apostrophe when one person or thing owns another.

> *Examples:* Superman saved his <u>friend's</u> house. ✓ (The friend owns the house, so you need an apostrophe.)
> Superman has two good <u>friend's</u>. ✗ (The friends own nothing in this sentence, so you don't need an apostrophe—*friends* is simply plural.)

PUNCTUATION—APOSTROPHE OF POSSESSION (cont.)

Where to put it

You have to remember only ONE thing about where to put the apostrophe of possession.

Put the apostrophe immediately after the person or thing that does the possessing.

Examples: A friend's house = the house of a <u>friend</u> → apostrophe goes after *friend* → friend's

My parents' house = the house of my <u>parents</u> → apostrophe goes after *parents* → parents'

The children's house = the house of the <u>children</u> → apostrophe goes after *children* → children's

That's it! No need to think about singulars and plurals. Just ask yourself: Who or what does the owning? *Then* put the apostrophe.

Insert the apostrophes where needed in these sentences. (Some sentences don't need any.)

a.   Phantoms horse is named Hero.

b.   Supermans best friends were Lois Lane and Jimmy Olsen.

c.   It was the three villains last attempt to get rid of Batman.

d.   Many childrens television shows have no real heroes.

e.   Adults usually admire the superheroes devotion to duty.

f.   The X-Mens fight against evil never seems to end.

g.   The films ending is a surprise.

h.   Fans can get more information about their superhero on the website.

i.   Batmans cave is beneath Gotham City.

j.   Many different actors have played Superman.

CAN YOU HELP?

This student's paragraph is missing all its capitalization and punctuation. Can you correct it?

superheroes can be our guides in everyday life most peoples lives even childrens lives involve tough decisions when faced with these decisions we can ask ourselves what would superman do I dont mean what special superpowers he would use but what choices he would make in the same situation superheroes have to make some very difficult decisions in do-or-die life-or-death situations of course their decisions might be more critical than the ones we have to make but they can still teach us something about the responsible way to act

PUZZLE TIME

① How many superhero words can you find in this wordsearch. The words might be the names of superheroes, their real identities, the villains they fight, or something to do with their special powers.

② How many words can you make using the letters from SPIDER-MAN? Write them on your own paper.

```
S P B Z R P H A N T O M P M
U R O B I N J V U L T U R E
P A F A K R Y P T O N I T E
E B A T G I R L B X E N A O
R P X M H D S L O M M U K J
W G E A H I O L K E B V F D
O E R N G U I K F N H G T S
M Q W P G O T H A M C I T Y
A X Z B S U P E R M A N L K
N G H J S P I D E R M A N H
W O L V E R I N E W V B A M
```

YOUR TURN TO WRITE

TIPS FOR SUPERSONIC, SUPER-POWERED WRITERS
Prepare for writing a discussion by brainstorming points for and against, without worrying too much about how strong or weak they are. Then look through them and choose two or three strong points to use in your discussion.

---

① Here are three entertainment topics. For each topic, brainstorm at least two arguments for and two arguments against, using the table below.

TOPIC	FOR	AGAINST
Are video and computer games good for children?		
Is reading a book better than seeing a film?		
Is Bart Simpson a good role model for children?		

② Now choose one topic and draft a discussion about it on the next page.
- State the issue clearly at the beginning.
- Organize your arguments into **for** and **against**.
- Write a topic sentence for each argument.
- Develop the arguments with examples and other details.
- Use connectives and "thread" words to link your arguments.
- Use modals and adverbs to show how strongly you feel.
- Say which side you agree with in your conclusion.

Revise your draft, checking for grammar, spelling, and punctuation, and then write it out again neatly on your own paper.

☀ YOUR TURN TO WRITE (cont.)

The issue _____

_____

_____

_____

Arguments for _____

_____

_____

_____

_____

_____

_____

_____

_____

_____

_____

_____

_____

Arguments against _____

_____

_____

_____

_____

_____

_____

_____

_____

_____

_____

_____

Your conclusion _____

_____

_____

This lesson aims to help you with school projects. It is organized differently from the other lessons in the book. It has three sections:

- Using your own words
- Writing imaginative texts based on facts
- Referencing

You will see how one student worked on a project on the topic of "Chinese Festivals and Customs," and you will do some work on this topic, too.

YOUR TURN TO WRITE

> **TIPS FOR PERFECTLY POLISHED PROJECT WRITERS**
>
> - Don't be tempted to just cut-and-paste from a web page to make your own text. You won't end up with a good piece of writing, and your teacher will be able to see it is not your own work.
>
> - Instead, select information and put it into your own words to show you understand what you are writing about.
>
> - Think about writing an imaginative text based on factual information—for example, a diary entry or a narrative—as well as factual reports and recounts.
>
> - Make sure you say exactly where you got your information. Write down the information of a book or website or other source as soon as you use it. This will save you from having to find it again at the end of your project for your bibliography.

☼ USING YOUR OWN WORDS

Here is some information about Chinese New Year that a student found on a website. Look below and on the next page to compare and see how he selected from the information and changed the words to make his own text. You don't have to read this text in detail—look mainly at the parts that have been marked.

CHINESE NEW YEAR

WHAT THE STUDENT DID

Chinese New Year starts with the New Moon on the first day of the new year and ends on the full moon 15 days later. The 15th day of the new year is called the *Lantern Festival*, which is celebrated at night with lantern displays and children carrying lanterns in a parade.

The Chinese calendar is based on a combination of lunar and solar movements. The lunar cycle is about 29.5 days. In order to "catch up" with the solar calendar, the Chinese insert an extra month every few years (seven years out of a 19-year cycle). This is the same as adding an extra day on a leap year. This is why, according to the solar calendar, the Chinese New Year falls on a different date each year.

Left out information he did not understand

New Year's Eve and New Year's Day are celebrated as a family affair, a time of reunion and thanksgiving. Ancestors are greatly respected in Chinese culture because they are responsible for laying the foundations for the fortune and glory of the family. Their presence is acknowledged on New Year's Eve with a dinner arranged for them at the family banquet table. The spirits of the ancestors, together with the living, celebrate the onset of the New Year as one great community. The communal feast is called "surrounding the stove" or "weilu." It symbolizes family unity and honors the past and present generations.

Left out some small details

The 15-day Celebration

Every day of the Lunar New Year has a special significance. The first day, for example, is the "welcoming of the gods of the heavens and earth." Many people abstain from meat on the first day of the new year because it is believed that this will ensure long and happy lives for them.

On the second day, the Chinese pray to their ancestors as well as to all the gods. They are extra kind to dogs and feed them well, as it is believed that the second day is the birthday of all dogs.

The fifth day is called "po woo." On that day people stay home to welcome the God of Wealth. No one visits families and friends on the fifth day because it will bring both parties bad luck. On the sixth to the tenth day, the Chinese visit their relatives and friends freely. They also visit the temples to pray for good fortune and health.

Selected from examples given—did not use all

The seventh day is considered the birthday of human beings. Noodles are eaten to promote longevity and raw fish for success.

The 10th day to the 12th are days that friends and relatives should be invited for dinner. After so much rich food, on the 13th day you should have simple rice congee and mustard greens (choi sum) to cleanse the system.

The 14th day should be for preparations to celebrate the Lantern festival, which is to be held on the 15th night.

Adapted from web page *Chinese New Year*, www.educ.uvic.ca/faculty/mroth/438/CHINA/Chinese_new_year.html

STUDENT'S TEXT

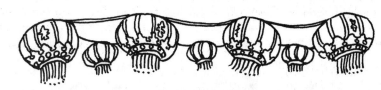

CHINESE NEW YEAR

WHAT THE STUDENT DID

> Wrote a sentence to introduce the topic

> Made up own sentences where needed

> Changed order of information

Chinese New Year is a very important time for Chinese people. It starts on the first New Moon of the year and begins a 15-day period of celebration until the Full Moon. The New Year falls on a different date each year because it is based on the Chinese calendar. This calendar is based on the movements of the sun and the moon.

Chinese people celebrate New Year's Eve and New Year's Day as a family affair. It is a time of reunion and thanksgiving. Ancestors, who are greatly respected in Chinese culture, are remembered on New Year's Eve with a dinner at the family banquet table. The spirits of the ancestors celebrate the New Year together with the living as one whole community. The communal feast is called "surrounding the stove," or "weilu" in Chinese, and is a symbol of family unity. (*Chinese New Year*, website)

> Used own words as much as possible

> Selected from examples given—did not use all

> Gave the name of the website—full details will be in the bibliography

Every day for 15 days after New Year's Day, there are rituals and celebrations of different kinds. For example, on the first day, people welcome the gods of heaven and earth. They do not eat meat because they believe it will give them long and happy lives. The fifth day is called "po woo," and people stay home to welcome the God of Wealth. Nobody visits anyone else because it will bring bad luck. The seventh day is considered to be the birthday of all humans. (*Chinese New Year*, website)

> Changed order of words

On the last day, the Lantern Festival is held at night. There are lantern displays everywhere and children carry lanterns in a parade.

> Added his own comment to end the report

Chinese New Year sounds like great fun and much more interesting than the Western way of celebrating.

✺ USING YOUR OWN WORDS (cont.)

① Read these three paragraphs about Chinese New Year from another website.* Complete the sentences about each using your own words. You may need to leave out some of the information.

a. *Of all the traditional Chinese festivals, the New Year was perhaps the most elaborate, colorful, and important. This was a time for the Chinese to congratulate each other and themselves on having passed through another year, a time to finish out the old, and to welcome in the new year.*

Chinese New Year is _____ of all Chinese festivals.

Chinese people _____

_____ and welcome

_____ .

b. *Preparations for the traditional Chinese New Year in old China started well before New Year's Day. The 20th of the Twelfth Moon (or month) was set aside for the annual housecleaning or the "sweeping of the grounds." After the house was cleaned, it was time to bid farewell to the Kitchen God or Zaowang—the guardian of the family hearth. By tradition, the Kitchen God left the house on the 23rd of the last month to report on the behavior of the family. At this time, the family did everything possible to obtain a good report from the Kitchen God. On the evening of the 23rd, they would give the Kitchen God a farewell dinner with sweet foods and honey.*

In the traditional Chinese New Year, preparations started well beforehand. One day was set aside for

_____ .

After this, the family _____ .

Everyone was very well behaved at this time because _____

_____ .

On the 23rd, they bid farewell to _____

_____ .

c. *In the Lantern Festival, people carried lanterns into the streets to take part in a great parade. Young men would highlight the parade with a dragon dance. The dragon was made of bamboo, silk, and paper and might stretch for more than 100 feet in length. The bobbing and the weaving of the dragon was an impressive sight, and it formed a fitting finish to the New Year festival.*

One of the _____ parts of the New Year was the _____ .

Everyone carried_____ and took part in

_____ . The highlight of the parade was

_____ . The dragon

_____ .

*Text on this page is adapted from *Traditional Celebration of the Chinese New Year*, Chinese Culture Center of San Francisco, www.c-c-c.org/culture-resources/holidays/traditional-celebration-of-the-chinese-new-year/

USING YOUR OWN WORDS (cont.)

② Read this interesting text about the Chinese animal zodiac. Then complete the shorter version below using the information and some of your own words.

The Chinese Animal Zodiac

The Chinese animal zodiac is a 12-year cycle used for dating the years. It represents a cyclical concept of time (based on the cycles of the moon), rather than the Western linear concept of time. Every year is assigned an animal name or "sign" according to a repeating cycle: Rat, Ox, Tiger, Rabbit, Dragon, Snake, Horse, Sheep (or Ram), Monkey, Rooster, Dog, and Pig (or Boar).

Horoscopes have developed around the animal signs, much like monthly horoscopes in the West have been developed for the different moon signs (Pisces, Aries, etc.). For example, a Chinese horoscope may predict that a person born in the Year of the Horse would be "cheerful, popular, and loves to compliment others."

According to Chinese legend, the 12 animals quarrelled one day as to who was to head the cycle of years. The gods were asked to decide and they held a contest: whoever was to reach the opposite bank of the river would be first, and the rest of the animals would receive their years according to their finish. All the 12 animals gathered at the river bank and jumped in. Unknown to the ox, the rat had jumped upon his back. As the ox was about to jump ashore, the rat jumped off the ox's back, and won the race. The pig, who was very lazy, ended up last. That is why the rat is the first year of the animal cycle, the ox second, and the pig last.

Which animal sign rules your birth year? What about other people you know?

Rat	1948	1960	1972	1984	1996	2008
Ox	1949	1961	1973	1985	1997	2009
Tiger	1950	1962	1974	1986	1998	2010
Rabbit	1951	1963	1975	1987	1999	2011
Dragon	1952	1964	1976	1988	2000	2012
Snake	1953	1965	1977	1989	2001	2013
Horse	1954	1966	1978	1990	2002	2014
Sheep	1955	1967	1979	1991	2003	2015
Monkey	1956	1968	1980	1992	2004	2016
Rooster	1957	1969	1981	1993	2005	2017
Dog	1958	1970	1982	1994	2006	2018
Boar	1959	1971	1983	1995	2007	2019

In the Chinese calendar, every year in a _____ is given an

_____, for example _____

_____. _____ have developed for these animal signs,

much like _____ for the different moon signs. For example,

_____ born in the Year of the Horse _____

_____. There is a _____ that

explains the order of the animal signs. The gods _____ to figure

out who should head the cycle of years. The rat used his cunning by _____

and won _____. The pig came last because _____.

That is why _____.

My animal sign is _____. What is _____?

☼ USING YOUR OWN WORDS (cont.)

> ### RESEARCH IDEA
> You might like to do some more research to find out what the animal means about your character and personality. If you are searching the Internet, you could type in "Chinese animal signs" or "year of the ___" (for whatever animal sign you are) in a search engine.

☼ WRITING IMAGINATIVE TEXTS BASED ON FACTS

It can be interesting to write imaginative kinds of texts based on factual information in school projects. For example, for this project, you could write a diary entry of someone's experiences over the New Year festival period.

Use the information from the previous texts and from the new text below to outline imaginative diary entries on the next page. Use the ideas given, but add ideas from your own imagination as well. Rewrite the entries on your own paper.

Traditional Taboos and Superstitions of Chinese New Year

House Cleaning

The entire house should be cleaned before New Year's Day. On New Year's Eve, all brooms, brushes, and other cleaning equipment are put away. Sweeping or dusting should not be done on New Year's Day for fear that good fortune will be swept away. After New Year's Day, the floors may be swept. There are many superstitions about the way to sweep. For example, if you sweep the dirt out over the threshold, you will sweep one of the family away. Also, to sweep the dust and dirt out of your house by the front entrance is to sweep away the good fortune of the family. All dirt and rubbish must be taken out the back door.

Bringing in the New Year and Expelling the Old

Shooting off firecrackers on New Year's Eve is the Chinese way of sending out the old year and welcoming in the new year. On the stroke of midnight on New Year's Eve, every door in the house, and even windows, have to be open to allow the old year to go out.

Personal Appearances and Cleanliness

On New Year's Day, we are not supposed to wash our hair because it would mean we would have washed away good luck for the new year. Red clothing is preferred during this festive occasion. Red is considered a bright, happy color, sure to bring the wearer a sunny and bright future. It is believed that appearance and attitude during New Year's Day sets the tone for the rest of the year. Children and unmarried friends, as well as close relatives, are given "lai see," little red envelopes with crisp one dollar bills inserted, for good fortune.

Adapted from *Taboos and Superstitions of Chinese New Year*, www.educ.uvic.ca/faculty/mroth/438/CHINA/taboos.html

☼ MY DIARY

- Sweeping of the grounds
- In trouble for sweeping the wrong way

Entry #1

_____
_____
_____
_____
_____

- Farewell to Kitchen God
- Everyone kind to each other
- Farewell dinner— yummy food

Entry #2

_____
_____
_____
_____
_____

- New Year's Eve
- Special dinner
- Honor ancestors
- Firecrackers

Entry #3

_____
_____
_____
_____
_____

- New Year's Day
- The Year of the
  _____
- Red clothes
- "Lai see" envelopes

Entry #4

_____
_____
_____
_____

- 7th day of New Year—everyone's birthday
- Everyone eats too much

Entry #5

_____
_____
_____
_____

- Lantern Festival
- Parade
- Dragon dance
- End of festival

Entry #6

_____
_____
_____
_____

✺ REFERENCING

It is very important to say where you got your information from (e.g., which book, which website, which newspaper article, etc.). This is called **referencing**.

You need to give a reference:

- when you quote **someone's exact words** AND when you put **someone else's information** into your own words
- **on the page** you use the information AND **in the bibliography** at the end.

The student who wrote about the Chinese New Year at the beginning of the lesson gave the name of the website that he got his information from: *Chinese New Year*, website.

- If he had known the name of the site's author, he would have written that instead of the title of the website.
- If he had used information from a book, he would have given just the author's last name and date (e.g., Brown, 2003).

In his bibliography, he gave the full details of the site.

Here is the student's full bibliography. (Note: The following references are for sample formatting purposes only. The information and dates are not accurate.)

Website
Website
Book
Book
Newspaper article

Alphabetical order
Date that website was written
Use title of website if no author is given
Date that you accessed the site
Title of article; Name of newspaper

"Celebration of the Chinese New Year." 23 January 2004. Chinese Culture Center of San Francisco. 5 May 2004. <www.c-c-c.org/culture-resources/holidays/traditional-celebration-of-the-chinese-new-year/>

"Chinese New Year," 12 March 2002. 7 May 2004. <www.educ.uvic.ca/faculty/mroth/438/CHINA/Chinese_new_year.html>

Grahame, Marty. The Chinese Zodiac. Sydney: Brown Publishing Company, 1995.

Jones, Jack and Luis King. Festivals of the World. Melbourne: Hector Publishing, 2001.

Larsen, Rose. "It's the Year of the Monkey," The Gazette 3 January 2004.

Can you write these materials as a bibliography? Use the lines on the next page.

A book called *Festivals* by Jenny Bilson, published in 1999 in London by Slater Publishing

A newspaper article titled "Which year were you born?" by Kyle Tyson, which appeared in the Northern News on January 10, 2004

A website called *Chinese Calendar* by Scotland Online, accessed on April 3, 2001 www.new-year.co.uk/chinese/calendar and written on September 15, 2000

A book called *Celebrating New Year's Around the World* by Eric Grant, published in 2002 in Los Angeles by Miller Publishing

REFERENCING (cont.)

_____

_____

_____

_____

_____

_____

_____

_____

_____

_____

YOUR TURN TO WRITE

You might be doing a research project at school right now. If so, keep this lesson close by to help you. If you are not working on a project, choose any topic you would like to research and write about. Perhaps you could research and write about the culture and customs of a country you are interested in. Jot down some of your ideas below.

ANSWER KEY

LESSON 1   PAGES 6-13

What did you read?
① **a.** two   **b.** Roald Amundsen
   c. He saw the Norwegian flag flying.
② bad—they were not suited for the long journey or the deep snow
③ **a.** exhausted   **b.** disappointed
④ the rations slowly ran out
⑤ His diary suggests that he knew they were going to die: "I do not think we can hope for any better things now."

How was it written?
① You should have checked: Who it is about; What job or position the person had; What the person had done before; What the person wanted to do; The period in which the events happened; Where the events took place
② **a.** In the early 20th century   **b.** In 1910
   c. from this point on   **d.** Three weeks later
④ You might have said something like: The diary was interesting and moving. It clearly showed the terrible way the men died. It also showed that Scott really was a hero—just as William says in his conclusion.

Spelling and meaning
② **a.** exploration   **b.** expedition
   c. ambition   **d.** devotion
③ **a.** courage   **b.** Hardship   **c.** perish
   d. blizzard   **e.** rations   **f.** obstacles
④ **a.** courageous   **b.** heroic   **c.** adventurous
   d. determined   **e.** extraordinary   **f.** bold
   g. experienced   **h.** brilliant   **i.** gallant or valiant

Grammar
Amelia Earhart was born in Kansas in the United States of America in 1898. She was just five years old when Orville and Wilbur Wright made their famous flight at Kitty Hawk in North Carolina. Little did she know then that she would be just as famous in the history of aviation as the Wright brothers. In 1932, Earhart flew out of New Brunswick, on the east coast of Canada, aiming for Paris. She wanted to be the first woman to successfully make a flight across the Atlantic Ocean. Unfortunately, a severe storm forced her to land in Ireland, rather than Paris, but she had still achieved her goal. Sadly, she died only five years later, as she attempted to be the first woman to circumnavigate the world. She encountered trouble over the Pacific Ocean, just east of the International Dateline, and disappeared. Thirty years later, the search for her plane was renewed. On a small island just south of the equator, a navigator's bookcase and part of a woman's shoe were found. It seems likely that they belonged to this very brave aviation pioneer.

Punctuation
① **a.** As a young boy, Ernest Shackleton longed for adventure and excitement.
   b. Despite all the hardships, they were determined to continue their voyage.
   c. After a slow journey through pack ice, their ship finally reached its destination.
   d. In 1778, Captain James Cook was the most famous explorer of his time.
   e. In 1871, David Livingstone, the greatest African explorer of all time, had been missing for six years.
   f. The *New York Herald* sent Henry Stanley, an experienced reporter, to find Livingstone.
② **a.** There were four dogs: Henry, Jacky, Nino, and Nina.
   b. He wrote, "I can't go on any further."
   c. The trip has three stages: sailing there, climbing the mountains, and setting up camp.
   d. Remember these things: travel in a group, let someone know your route, and take a safety kit.
   e. His first words were, "Welcome to you all."

Can you help?
   a. 1   **b.** 5   **c.** 2   **d.** 3   **e.** 6   **f.** 7   **g.** 4

Puzzle time

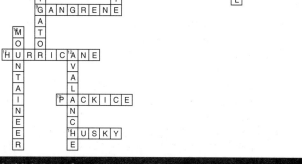

LESSON 2   PAGES 14-20

What did you read?
① because she claims that three relatives had died in Aunt Bessie's care
② a sign of danger approaching
③ c
④ to ask her to call and keep her aunt on the phone so that she could get rid of the meal
⑤ being read a bedtime story that is for much younger children
⑥ c

#8074 Write from the Start! Writing Lessons   88   ©Teacher Created Resources, Inc.

How was it written?
① Answers may vary.
② Aunt Bessie hugging her (suffocating her), feeding her (poisoning her), reading to her (torturing her)
③ **a.** thundering **b.** sliced **c.** rattled
   d. grasped **e.** mounted **f.** slipped
④ **a.** The idea of a terrifying death sliced through my heart like a cold, sharp blade.
   b. A definite sign!
   c. What would Charlie's Angels do in a situation like this?
   d. Horror of horrors!

Spelling and meaning
① **a.** squirmed **b.** situation, responsible
   c. alert **d.** announced **e.** oblivious
   f. obviously, accident **g.** crippling
   h. stomach
② **a.** legs **b.** heart **c.** knees **d.** blood
   e. throats **f.** face **g.** ears

Grammar
① **a.** (Bianca) babysits her little sister, Yoli, every afternoon.
   b. (My Uncle Ernie) always calls during our favorite TV program.
   c. (You) can watch the nature documentary.
   d. (He) talks for a very long time.
   e. Sometimes (she) is very naughty.
   f. (Sasha and Julia) stay with their cousins in the country every Christmas.
   g. (You) can go to bed right now.
   h. (Their cousins) never come to visit them in the city.
② **b/d:** My Uncle Ernie always calls during our favorite TV program, and he talks for a very long time.
   c/g: You can watch the nature documentary, or you can go to bed right now.
   f/h: Sasha and Julia stay with their cousins in the country every Christmas, but their cousins never come to visit them in the city.
③ **a.** My Aunty Dora makes soup that smells like rotten fish.
   b. I can hardly breathe when my Uncle Vinnie gives me his famous bear hugs.
   c. I love my great grandmother because she tells funny stories.
   d. My cousins and I end up fighting every time we get together.
   e. Mom always gives us a lecture about being polite before we visit our Aunty Zita.

Puzzle time
The Artful Dodger: *Oliver Twist*
Christopher Robin: *Winnie the Pooh*
Peter, Susan, Edmund, and Lucy: *The Lion, the Witch, and the Wardrobe*
Dorothy: *The Wizard of Oz*
The Oompa Loompas: *Charlie and the Chocolate Factory*
The Lost Boys: *Peter Pan*
The Mad Hatter: *Alice's Adventures in Wonderland*
Mole, Rat, Badger, and Toad: *The Wind in the Willows*
Miss Trunchbull: *Matilda*

LESSON 3   PAGES 21–28

What did you read?
① b
② drifting
③ When you cook, you make things hotter. When you put on blankets, you get hotter. So maybe the heat from the blankets would "cook" dreams.
④ a
⑤ the sound of wind as the rider rides
⑥ (Possible answers) "I Lie Straight": content, happy, peaceful; "Drifting Off": sleepy, happy, calm; "My Bike": excited, happy, free

How were they written?
① **a.** brushes, floats down, settles
   b. swooping, flying
② **a.** a whisper **b.** a fox **c.** a boat
③ **a.** i. dusk ii. smooth path iii. tires hum iv. no hands v. tailwind
   b. speed

Spelling and meaning
① **a.** through **b.** threw **c.** straight **d.** strait
   e. cot **f.** caught
② **c.** breeze, straight, search, possums, through, swooping, tires, bruises, quiet, caught, curled, smooth
③ Possible answers:
   a. whack—a newspaper hitting something, a smack
   b. wham—a boxer falling to the floor
   c. wheeze—a person breathing hard
   d. whimper—a child crying, a dog crying
   e. whine—a person complaining
   f. whinny—a horse sound
   g. whip—the wind
   h. whirr—helicopter blades
   i. whiz—a fast ride on a roller coaster
   j. whoop—children playing a game, a bird's cry

Grammar
② Possible answers:
   a. The wind is a whip.
   b. Sleep is a soft cocoon.
   c. Dancing is freedom.
   d. Chocolate cake is heaven.
   e. Exams are torture.

Punctuation

① There is not one right answer, because it is your response to the poem. However, you might have said:
   a. smooth, flowing
   b. The punctuation makes you read it in a way that reflects the sheet falling.
   c. because the feeling does not end; to keep the peaceful, dreamy feeling

② Again, there is not one right answer, but you might have said:
   a. quickly
   b. The punctuation makes you read it in a way that reflects the bike riding.
   c. It emphasises the excitement.

③ There is not one right answer, but here is one way to punctuate "Summer at the Pool":
   Splash!
   Down down,
   straighten out now,
   What a dive!
   Sweet, sweet, coolness
   up now up,
   floating like driftwood
   thick silent peace
   mmmm.
   Splash!
   Peace over,
   time for fun!

Puzzle time

a. Wee Willie Winkie
b. three little kittens
c. Jack and Jill
d. Little Miss Muffet
e. an old woman
f. Humpty Dumpty
g. Little Bo Peep
h. the mouse
i. this little piggy
j. the cow

LESSON 4 — PAGES 29-35

What did you read?

① b

② Level 1: services like sewage, water, electricity, air conditioning, and gas; Level 2: factories and storage; Level 3: living area

③ **a.** sides of a cardboard box   **b.** Styrofoam
   c. dark blue tissue paper   **d.** thin rubber tubing
   e. bubble wrap   **f.** Easter-egg packaging
   g. plastic sheeting
   h. clear plastic cookie packaging

④ **a.** False   **b.** True   **c.** False

How was it written?

① **a.** first paragraph   **b.** second paragraph

② ORDER; We started; The first level; Then we worked on the second level; Next, we made the third level; Finally

③ **a.** The students did not think tall skyscrapers would be suitable out at sea.
   b. They did not think cars would be used in a sea-city.

④ positive

Spelling and meaning

① **a.** basic, basis, basement
   b. electric, electrical, electrify
   c. unreal, unrealistic, reality

② **a.** lightweight   **b.** approximately   **c.** silos
   d. skyscrapers   **e.** basically   **f.** height
   g. design   **h.** materials   **i.** electricity
   j. realistic   **k.** vehicles   **l.** decided
   m. measuring   **n.** cylinders

③ **a.** whether   **b.** weather   **c.** allowed
   d. aloud   **e.** which   **f.** witch   **g.** piece
   h. peace   **i.** board   **j.** bored

Grammar

① In class, we <u>were asked to construct</u> a bridge out of paper that <u>could hold up</u> as much weight as possible. The bridge <u>had to span</u> a distance of 4 inches. Chris Learned's was the best. Chris <u>managed to hold up</u> 2.2 pounds without his paper collapsing. Other students who <u>tried to hold up</u> 2.2 pounds failed because of their design. Chris <u>made</u> his bridge with a section shaped like an unused staple. Our bridge <u>held up</u> 14 ounces, which <u>was</u> the second-largest weight.

② **a.** glue, tape, fix   **b.** build, construct
   c. begin, commence   **d.** rotate, twist, invert
   e. place, stand   **f.** view, observe

Punctuation

a. oddly-shaped   **b.** ice-cold, red-hot
c. multi-story   **d.** eight-tenths
e. mid-February   **f.** life-like

Can you help?

a. 2   **b.** 5   **c.** 1   **d.** 6   **e.** 3   **f.** 7   **g.** 8   **h.** 4

Puzzle time

① **a.** spherical   **b.** conical   **c.** cubic
   d. octagonal   **e.** hexagonal   **f.** pentagonal

② **a.** Atlantis   **b.** Neptune   **c.** Poseidon

LESSON 5 — PAGES 36-43

What did you read?

① Joe wants Ms. Nori to help get a skateboard park built in his area.

② c

③ b

④ five

⑤ There is no one correct answer, although you might think his last point would be the most persuasive for Ms. Nori, who would be thinking of the whole community, not just young people.

⑥ Any of the following answers: It was designed by local skateboarders. / It is a place where big kids help little kids learn to skateboard. / It is safe.

How was it written?
① c
② Perhaps because he thinks it is an especially good reason, and also because it sums up all his other arguments.
③ b
④ c
⑤ There is no one correct answer, but you might say yes, because the letter was clear, or because it was polite and friendly, or because Joe showed how strongly he felt and how much he loved skateboarding.

Spelling and meaning
① **a.** their   **b.** They're   **c.** There   **d.** there
e. They're, their, there
② **a.** ungrateful   **b.** insignificant   **c.** unselfish
d. immobile   **e.** imperfect   **f.** impersonal
g. impolite   **h.** unimpressive   **i.** inactive
j. inadequate   **k.** indirect   **l.** ineffective
③ Possible answers:
a. snowboard, surfboard, skateboard, boardroom, cardboard, chalkboard
b. snowflake, snowboard, snowboarder, snowball, snowdrift, snowfall, snowfield
c. surfboard, surfboat, channel-surf, windsurf
d. windbreak, windburn, windblown, windchill, windbreaker, windmill, windsurf, windshield, windswept, windjammer, tradewind, downwind

Grammar
① **a.** sensible   **b.** beautiful   **c.** brilliant
d. entertaining   **e.** boring
② GOOD: positive, brilliant, useful, excellent, clever; BAD: useless, unhelpful, shocking, negative, harmful; BEAUTIFUL: glorious, gorgeous, attractive, splendid, magnificent; UGLY: unattractive, revolting, unpleasant, terrible, disgusting

Punctuation
① **a.** I believe <u>it's</u> a really terrible plan.
b. The group wants you to know <u>its</u> honest opinion.
c. Most people who object to <u>its</u> construction don't know the facts.
d. One thousand people say <u>it's</u> an excellent place for a skatepark.
e. <u>Its</u> success will depend on <u>its</u> size, <u>its</u> design, and <u>its</u> location.
f. <u>It's</u> been talked about for long enough. <u>It's</u> time for action.

Can you help?
a. 2   **b.** 5   **c.** 4   **d.** 3   **e.** 1

Puzzle time

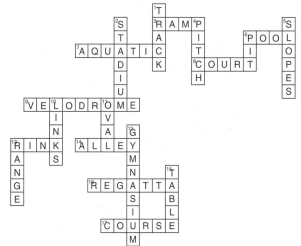

Your turn to write
Possible answers:
① **a.** local newspaper, local council member or mayor
b. local newspaper; local council member or mayor
c. local or major newspaper
d. local or major newspaper; government official
e. school district superintendent; principal
f. principal; school district superintendent; local newspaper

LESSON 6   PAGES 44-49

What did you read?
① **a.** False   **b.** False   **c.** True   **d.** False
e. True
② hydrogen bombs
③ how hot they are
④ light years
⑤ b

How was it written?
① c
② The words **star** and **stars** are used 22 times (23 if you count the title of the report).
③ **a.** What are Stars?   **b.** Our Sun
c. How They Die
④ headings, paragraphs, topic sentences
⑤ because they are personal comments and opinions, and these are not relevant in an information report where the focus should be on facts
⑥ These words are defined: light years, supernovae, black holes. You might have wanted the author to define any of the other words, but perhaps an explanation of the word "nuclear" is the one that would most help readers. (It is probably not defined because it would be very difficult to define it in a few simple words.)

Spelling and meaning

① **a.** enormous **b.** powerful **c.** spectacular
   d. massive **e.** unimaginable **f.** temperature
② **a.** rotate **b.** million **c.** gravity
   d. difference **e.** collapse
③ **a.** phenomenon—an observable fact or event
   b. phantom—ghostly apparition
   c. phase—stage in a process
   d. philosopher—a person who seeks wisdom or enlightenment
   e. phoenix—imaginary bird in ancient stories
   f. phony—fake, unreal
   g. prophet—someone who predicts the future
   h. phrase—short group of words
   i. sphere—round, three-dimensional object or shape
   j. trophy—prize or award
④ **a.** botanist **b.** biologist **c.** geologist
   d. physicist **e.** chemist

Grammar

Corrections are underlined:
b. Meteors are sometimes called "shooting stars," but <u>they are</u> not really <u>stars</u>.
c. Some meteors are colored—mostly blue and white, though <u>they</u> might sometimes be red or green.
d. A communication satellite <u>bounces</u> signals from one point on Earth to another point.
e. Galaxies are vast clusters of thousands of millions of stars. <u>They are</u> classified according to <u>their</u> shape.
f. Telescopes magnify distant objects in the night sky. <u>They use</u> lenses and mirrors to make things appear closer and larger.

Punctuation

a. Earth is the third planet from the Sun (which is 93 million miles away).
b. Venus (named after the Roman goddess of love) is Earth's closest neighbor.
c. Venus is also the closest in size to Earth (only 405 miles less in diameter).
d. Venus spins from west to east (opposite to Earth).
e. Venus is the hottest planet in the solar system (around 870 degrees Fahrenheit).

Can you help?

People used to think comets were fireballs, but that is not correct. <u>They are actually frozen, lifeless bodies most of the time.</u> They have solid centers of dirty ice surrounded by gas. <u>They only come to life when they come near the Sun,</u> because the Sun heats them up and releases gases trapped inside. These gases form the tails of comets. The tails of comets can be millions of kilometers long—it is really only because of <u>their tails</u> that we see comets at all. Comets orbit the Sun just like planets, but <u>their orbits</u> are far greater and so <u>they last</u> much longer. Some take thousands of years

to complete their orbit. The most famous comet is Halley's Comet, which comes around about every 76 years. The last time was in 1986, and it is expected to return in 2061.

Puzzle time

① **a.** Mars **b.** comet **c.** astronaut
   d. Jupiter **e.** meteorite **f.** Venus
   g. Saturn **h.** Uranus **i.** Neptune
   j. Mercury **k.** Earth **l.** galaxy
② universe

LESSON 7   PAGES 50-56

What did you read?

① The soldier is drinking and then sleeping; the boy is fishing.
② convicts and soldiers; The convicts are walking off the ship, and the soldiers are keeping them moving and in line.
③ **a.** He is writing and that would be unusual to many of the people in the scene—that is, they may not be able to read or write themselves.
   b. The convicts would have been below deck on their long voyage.
   c. the equator; Crossing the equator was a very important event, and the convicts were probably allowed on deck. This would have been the last time they had seen the sky.
   d. They have been on the ship for a very long time—about six months—and their legs are more used to a moving surface than to the stable ground.
   e. Perhaps because David is free and the convict boy is not.
④ **a.** paragraph 2 **b.** paragraph 1

How was it written?

① interesting, three
② **a.** strangely quiet **b.** stamp up and down . . . shouting at the convicts . . . their tone is rough and angry
③ **a.** flopped, squirming, gasping **b.** stagger, stumble, clutching **c.** stamp, shouting, pushing **d.** thrusts, twists

Spelling and meaning

① **a.** wretches **b.** thrusts **c.** gesture
   d. pitiful **e.** wanders, clutching
   f. stagger, stumble **g.** soldier, rough
   h. Although, wrapped **i.** swig, promptly
② **a.** shuffle, hobble **b.** glide **c.** pace
   d. march, dash **e.** stamp, lumber
   f. glide, twist **g.** prowl, pace
   h. hobble, stagger **i.** totter **j.** scurry
   k. slither, glide

Grammar

① **a.** Their hair is knotted [with] dirt and straw.
   b. The trip [across] the oceans was harsh and long.

c. Many [of] the women [by] the docks were carrying small children.

d. Children played quite happily [on] the pebbly shore.

e. I felt sick [with] grief and loneliness.

f. Travelers led their weary horses [to] the water troughs [outside] the public house.

Punctuation

a. The boys, hoping to reach the top by sundown, pushed on in the fading light.

b. A small girl, hat tucked under her arm, smiled shyly at us.

c. There are ten men in the room, all sitting around a small table, and they look up as we enter.

d. My uncle, usually a rough-spoken man, gently asked the boy his name.

e. The swimmers, exhausted by their adventure, flung themselves onto the riverbank.

f. The students playing near the basketball courts are in trouble. (none needed)

g. The small children, kept awake by the noise, huddled together under the blankets.

h. The old man, his eyes flashing angrily, refused to move.

i. The boy looking this way is the thief. (none needed)

Can you help?

I am **sitting** here in a café in the town square **waiting** for a parade to begin. **Although** the day is **extremely** cold, the crowd is huge. **Everyone** is very **excited** and very noisy as they wait for the parade to start. I can **hear** trumpets and drums; the parade has begun. **L**eading the parade are **people** on stilts **wearing** bright-colored hats and **flowing** capes. **O**ne **stumbles** for a second before steadying up and continuing on. **T**he **crowd** cheers. **T**he stilt-walkers are **followed** by some very small **children. T**heir faces are painted with **animal** masks**,** and they are **clutching** balloons in their hands. **N**ow I can see young **girls** in bodysuits doing **cartwheels** and tumbles. **T**he **scene** changes every minute. **E**ach time a new group appears, the crowd shouts out and cheers wildly. **T**he biggest cheer is given to the town band at the end of the parade and to a little boy playing a very big drum**.**

Puzzle time

a. baggage   b. jetty   c. deck
d. passenger   e. anchor   f. mast
g. porthole   h. captain

LESSON 8   PAGES 57-64

What did you read?

① she disagrees
② a. people, animals

b. to give humans pleasure by showing them animals they would not otherwise see

c. education, conservation, and research

③ b

④ Sumatran orangutan/black rhinoceros

How was it written?

① The introduction is quite clear, but she changed it to make the start of her talk more interesting and to catch her listeners' attention.

② a

③ zoos and research 5, purpose of zoos today 2, zoos and education 3, purpose of zoos in the past 1, zoos and conservation 4

④ five

Spelling and meaning

① a. cruel (this word can also be pronounced with two syllables)

b. survives, species, modern, believe, purpose, pleasure, research

c. certainly, protection, endangered

d. disappearing, conservation, captivity

e. international, 5

② a. century b. science c. excellent, exceptions d. Recently, celebrated

③ pleasure, satisfaction; vanish, disappear; aim, purpose; certainly, definitely; merciless, cruel; research, study; endangered, threatened; modern, recent; display, exhibition; benefit, advantage

④ a. endangered b. research c. captivity
d. species e. believe f. international

Grammar

a. However b. for example c. As a result
d. Nevertheless e. Firstly, Secondly

Punctuation

② Possible answer:

In the past, zoos were exhibition parks. Their <u>only</u> purpose was to give humans pleasure, by showing them wonderful, exotic creatures that they would otherwise <u>never</u> see. Because animals were <u>only</u> there for the benefit of humans like you and me, no one took much care of them. They were transported <u>thousands</u> of miles around the world, then locked up in small, bare, lonely cages. In those days, zoos <u>were</u> cruel.

These days, things are <u>very different</u>. The whole <u>purpose</u> of zoos has changed. Now zoos have <u>three</u> major purposes: education, conservation, and research. They aim to make animals better off everywhere. Because of this, the way animals are cared for is also different.

Can you help?

a. 5 b. 4 c. 1 d. 3 e. 6 f. 2

Puzzle time

```
R B P E Q B W R E T R J I K H C Z I O P L F S
F W U R H A B I T A T T V H G F E Q E A I B M
U R E I N M L D R E W N U O T Y B V E H Y U
E N D A N G E R E D X S D F L A I T B N Y I L
I L B P S R P O P U L A T I O N R T Y B V E W
P U Y G S Z X I O L F I T Y U R E S E A R C H
P R C M O A L B C E W R F F A S L R B F E O U
A O X N G R P R O T E C T E D U T R A T H W R
R Q A E L O Q E N T Y O D S A G B K G B T M O
K W R C T K I E T R T N T Y N I A Q M N L D B
S Y T R H L Y D R T Y S P E C I E S T R S E T
Q U U T R I Z I O R E E T Y F F X S D X K L I
L P I O E Y N N L R F R D G H J T L J H A P K
O K P G A Q A G R T A V A T S G I T Y U B V F
R S O F T W F M E G P A R F H U N T I N G K J
T A A S U D D G W Z G T H K G O C Q W E T H F
B E C D Y G H F Q F O I T J F I T A L H P R O
V F O Y Q M T S P S G O E Q A E M L T G I R E
W G L F P B L A M K D N A T U R E P E Q T U A
```

LESSON 9 — PAGES 65-71

What did you read?

① underwater earthquake, volcano, hurricanes, underwater landslides
② **a.** False **b.** True **c.** True
③ a break in Earth's crust
④ small earthquakes
⑤ a

How was it written?

① **Tsunamis** are freakishly large waves which are usually formed when the seabed is disturbed by an underwater earthquake or by a volcano. An **earthquake** is when there is a trembling or vibration (a "quake") of Earth's surface.
② **a.** end of paragraph 1
  b. i. end of paragraph 2
    ii. after the second sentence of paragraph 3
④ There is no right answer, but you might have said that diagrams would have helped. They usually do help the reader understand explanations.

Spelling and meaning

① catastrophic, caused, destructive, disturbed, earthquake, eruption, friction, hurricanes, landslides, livestock, occurs, shallower, tremors, vibration, volcano
② **a.** Landslides **b.** caused **c.** disturbed
  d. eruption **e.** tremors **f.** friction
③ **a.** disastrous (disaster)
  b. tragic (tragedy)
  c. destructive (destruction)
  d. terrible (terror)
  e. horrific (horror)
  f. shocking (shock)
  g. devastating (devastation)
  h. calamitous (calamity)
④ **a.** origami **b.** kimono **c.** karate **d.** karaoke

Grammar

b. The tremors were felt by people living in tall buildings.
c. Seismographs are used by scientists to measure vibrations.
d. The main quake is sometimes followed by smaller aftershocks.
e. Waves up to 33-feet high were triggered by two earthquakes on the seabed.
f. The Richter Scale is used by seismologists to measure earthquakes.
g. Earthquake "hot spots" have been identified by scientists.

Punctuation

At the back end of a glacier, high up in the mountains, is a large basin called the "neve." The neve is where the snow builds up and gets packed in ice. The long, middle part of the glacier is called the "trunk." The ice from the neve slowly flows downhill and adds to the trunk of the glacier. Eventually, ice from the trunk arrives at the front end of the glacier—the "terminal." This is where the glacier melts and comes out as a stream or river. As the glacier moves downhill it moves over humps and around bends in the valley. This causes the glacier ice to crack and buckle. The cracks formed are called "crevasses." When the glacier flows down a steep drop, an "icefall" is formed. An icefall is like a waterfall but is made of glacier ice.

Can you help?

Glaciers are like huge rivers of ice that come sliding down from the mountains. High up in the Alps, layers and layers of snow build up and get pressed together into ice. As the ice gets heavier and heavier, it starts to slide downhill. This moving ice is called a "glacier." Sometimes glaciers gradually expand and move forwards down the valleys into the sea, but at other times they gradually shrink and move backwards up into the mountains. When the front end of a glacier moves forwards, we say it is "advancing;" and when it moves backwards, we say it is "retreating."

Puzzle time

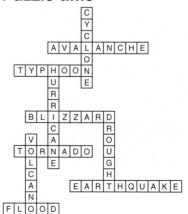

LESSON 10   PAGES 72-78

What did you read?
① a
② a. Children can aim for the same high moral standards.
   b. They fight for good, no matter how hopeless things look.
   c. Any of these answers: Real-life heroes are not particularly strong or brave. / Real-life heroes don't have special powers. / Real-life heroes don't always win.
③ d
④ for the question

How was it written?
① how long, names
② to show that the writer has given equal thought to both sides; the discussion is balanced
③ a
④ another (para. 3), many other (para. 4), another thing (para. 6), also (para. 7)
⑤ You would probably check all of these—all help to make the discussion quite clear.

Spelling and meaning
① a. whole   b. benefits   c. ridiculous
   d. drawbacks   e. perfect   f. qualities
   g. moral   h. mutants   i. particularly
   j. standards   k. prejudice   l. balance
② a. tomatoes   b. potatoes   c. volcanoes
   d. echoes   e. mosquitoes   f. torpedoes
   g. mangoes   h. heroes

③
FOR	AGAINST
Advantages	Disadvantages
Pluses	Minuses
Positives	Negatives
Benefits	Drawbacks
Affirmative case	Negative case

Grammar
a. The Phantom is definitely the best superhero ever. 1
   The Phantom is probably the best superhero ever. 2
   The Phantom may be the best superhero ever. 3
b. We should encourage children to watch films like *Spider-Man*. 2
   We must encourage children to watch films like *Spider-Man*. 1
   We could encourage children to watch films like *Spider-Man*. 3
c. Children could copy the behavior of superheroes. 2
   Children are sure to copy the behavior of superheroes. 1
   Children might possibly copy the behavior of superheroes. 3
d. Parents should always stop children from watching these shows. 1
   Perhaps parents should stop children from watching these shows. 3
   Parents should probably stop children from watching these shows. 2

Punctuation
a. Phantom's horse is named Hero.
b. Superman's best friends were Lois Lane and Jimmy Olsen.
c. It was the three villains' last attempt to get rid of Batman.
d. Many children's television shows have no real heroes.
e. Adults usually admire the superheroes' devotion to duty.
f. The X-Men's fight against evil never seems to end.
g. The film's ending is a surprise.
h. Fans can get more information about their superhero on the website. (none needed)
i. Batman's cave is beneath Gotham City.
j. Many different actors have played Superman. (none needed)

Can you help?
Superheroes can be our guides in everyday life. Most people's lives, even children's lives, involve tough decisions. When faced with these decisions, we can ask ourselves, "What would Superman do?" I don't mean what special superpowers he would use, but what choices he would make in the same situation? Superheroes have to make some very difficult decisions in do-or-die, life-or-death situations. Of course, their decisions might be more critical than the ones we have to make, but they can still teach us something about the responsible way to act.

Puzzle time
①
```
S P B Z R P H A N T O M P M
U R O B I N J V U L T U R E
P A F A K R Y P T O N I T E
E B A T G I R L B X E N A O
R P X M H D S L O M M U K J
W G E A H I O L K E B V F D
O E R N G U I K F N H G T S
M Q W P G O T H A M C I T Y
A X Z B S U P E R M A N L K
N G H J S P I D E R M A N H
W O L V E R I N E W V B A M
```

② man, spider, ram, mar, dam, pram, dram, mad, sad, sand, ride, side, spied, dire, sire, rise, near, dear, pear, pare, dare, mare, spare, spire, main, rain, drain, pain, sane, mane, pane, spear, pride, pries, prime, prim, dream, dries, drip, spread, smear, mine, reins, remind, drapes, snare (you might have found others)

LESSON 11 PAGES 79-87

Using your own words
① Possible answers:

a. Chinese New Year is <u>one of the most elaborate, colorful, and important</u> of all Chinese festivals. Chinese people <u>congratulate one another on getting through another year</u> and welcome <u>in the New Year</u>.

b. In the traditional Chinese New Year, preparations started well beforehand. One day was set aside for <u>the annual housecleaning, or "sweeping of the grounds."</u> After this, the family <u>bid farewell to the Kitchen God or Zaowang</u>. Everyone was very well behaved at this time because <u>the Kitchen God would report on the family's behavior</u>. On the 23rd, they bid farewell to <u>the Kitchen God with a special dinner</u>.

c. One of the <u>best</u> parts of the New Year was the <u>Lantern Festival</u>. Everyone carried <u>lanterns into the streets</u> and took part in <u>a parade</u>. The highlight of the parade was <u>the dragon dance</u>. The dragon <u>was made of bamboo, silk, and paper and could be 100 feet long</u>.

② Possible answer:

In the Chinese calendar, every year in a <u>12-year cycle</u> is given an <u>animal name</u>, for example, <u>Rat, Ox, Tiger, Rabbit, and Dragon.</u> <u>Horoscopes</u> have developed for these animal signs, much like <u>horoscopes in the West</u> for the different moon signs. For example, <u>a person</u> born in the Year of the Horse <u>is thought to be "cheerful, popular and loves to compliment others."</u> There is a <u>Chinese legend</u> that explains the order of the animal signs. The gods <u>held a race across a river</u> to figure out who should head the cycle of years. The rat used his cunning by <u>jumping on the back of the ox</u> and won <u>the race</u>. The pig came last because <u>he was very lazy</u>. That is why <u>the rat is the first year of the animal cycle and the pig last</u>. My animal sign is _____. What is <u>yours</u>?

Referencing
Bilson, Jenny. <u>Festivals</u>. London: Slater Publishing, 1999.

"Chinese Calendar." 15 September 2000. Scotland Online. 3 April 2001. <www.new-year.co.uk/Chinese/calendar>

Grant, Eric. <u>Celebrating New Year's Around the World</u>. Los Angeles: Miller Publishing, 2002.

Tyson, Kyle. "Which year were you born?" <u>Northern News</u> 10 January 2004.